SKE

Des Lavelle of Valentia, County Kerry, is a man of marine passions, and the beautiful Skellig Islands are listed ahead of the rest. A seaman, photographer, diving instructor and author, he – with his venerable boat, the *Béal Bocht* – has guided many thousands of visitors to the Skelligs. Allied to this activity, his summer days are spent personally appreciating the wonders of wildlife, archaeology and history that occupy every nook and cranny on Skellig – above and beneath the sea – and he has spent many winters taking these topics on a lecture circuit that stretches from mainland Europe to the west coast of the United States. His photographs and texts also form the core of the Skellig Experience Visitor Centre on Valentia.

Though now retired from commercial boating, the call of the Skellig still draws him, on special summer days, to his Lorelei in the Atlantic Ocean.

SKELLIG

EXPERIENCE THE EXTRAORDINARY

THE O'BRIEN PRESS
DUBLIN

This revised and updated edition published 2019
First published 1976 as *The Skellig Story* by The O'Brien Press Ltd,
12 Terenure Road East, Rathgar, Dublin 6, Ireland.
Tel: +353 1 4923333; Fax: +353 1 4922777
E-mail: books@obrien.ie
Website: www.obrien.ie
First paperback edition 1987.
Updated paperback edition published 1993.
Reprinted 1999. Revised edition published 2004.
Reprinted 2006, 2010, 2015.
The O'Brien Press is a member of Publishing Ireland.

ISBN: 978-1-78849-083-2

05 04 03 02 01
23 22 21 20 19

Typesetting, editing, layout and design: The O'Brien Press Ltd
Front and back cover photos: Des Lavelle

Printed and bound in Poland by Białostockie Zakłady Graficzne S.A.
The paper in this book is produced using pulp from managed forests.

Published in:

DUBLIN
UNESCO
City of Literature

'... both the Skelligs are pinnacled, crocketed, spired, arched, caverned, minaretted; and these gothic extravagances are not curiosities of the islands: they are the islands: there is nothing else'

GEORGE BERNARD SHAW

ACKNOWLEDGEMENTS

The author has been helped along over the years by many people, and would like to thank in particular the following:

Miss M. O'Brien, Librarian, Cahersiveen; Miss K. Turner, Kerry County Library; Mr T. Armitage, Central Library; Mr F.J. Ryan, Skerries; Mr T. Shortt, Cahersiveen; Mr J. Shanahan, Portmagee; Mr T. 'Busty' Burns, Valentia; Mr P. O'Sullivan, CBS, Cahersiveen; Mr J. O'Reilly, Cork; Mr A. Lidstrom, Umea, Sweden; Mr P. Gallagher, Hon. Secretary, Valentia Lifeboat; Mr L Houlihan, Engineer, Valentia Lifeboat, for facilitating access to Station logbooks; Mr Don Roberts, Kilkenny; The Secretary, Irish Wildbird Conservancy; Mr. P. Evans, Mr. O. Merne and Mr. A. Lack, for bird-counts and plant-lists of the first edition and to Mr S. Newton, Mr A. Walsh, Mr O. Merne and Mr. D. Tierney for current bird-counts; The Secretary, the Inspector, Marine Superintendent, and the Engineer-in-Chief, Irish Lights; Mr E. Lehane, Operations and Property Manager, Irish Lights; The Skellig Lighthouse Principal and Assistant Keepers of many dates; Mr R. Foran and Mr P. Stewart of Skellig lighthouse maintenance crew; The Board of Trinity College, Dublin; The Officers of the Royal Irish Academy; The Librarian, Bodleian Library, Oxford; The Archivist, Dept. of Irish Folklore, UCD, and the Directors of the National Museums of Dublin, Copenhagen and Oslo.

Initial Photographic and darkroom facilities and much valuable advice on that subject were given by Padraig Kennelly, Tralee, and Robin Holder, Valentia Island.

ABOUT THE PHOTOGRAPHS

All the photographs – except where otherwise accredited – are by the author, shot over the years since 1972 – initially with a Pentax Spotmatic and three lenses, 28mm, 50mm and 135mm, and later with a Nikon FG and two zoom lenses, 36/70mm and 70/120mm. The film used initially was whatever South Kerry's limited supplies offered – a sinful mixture of Kodak Tri X, Plus X, Kodachrome, Ektachrome, Fujichrome and Agfachrome – as well as Kodacolor negative, which was coerced to yield black-and-white prints. In summer 2003 a digital Fuji Finepix 3800 joined the camera bag. And today, the Skellig photo files keep growing apace – now courtesy of the ubiquitous iPhone!

CONTENTS

FOREWORD

The Skellig Islands are many times more important than either their size or location would suggest. In any world map of archaeology, the Skellig stands out in bold, conspicuous letters; similarly, in the ornithological world, the name of Skellig conveys a richness of seabird life that is not easily equaled.

And there is more: fascinating lighthouse history, magnificent cliff scenery, interesting local folklore, incredible richness in the surrounding ocean ... and the many, many Skellig questions that do not have answers.

But that is only part of the motivation for this book; the real reason is that these Skellig Islands continue to fascinate me – even after some seventy-five years of visitations. I have sailed around them, flown over them and dived on every sheer underwater cliff face beneath them; I have visited them in childhood and perhaps fifty times each year from 1968 to 2014 to wander and wonder, and by researching, writing and poring over a wide variety of photographs, I can be out there immediately in spirit, savouring, as George Bernard Shaw said about the place, 'the magic that takes you out, far out, of this time and this world.'

These spiritual visits are too wonderful to hide; but one must try to strike a balance of interest for the historian, the bird-lover, the archaeology student, the Kerryman who hungers for more knowledge of his native ground and for that day-visitor who seeks a jolt of fantasy in his life.

Elsewhere in the book I have named the many individuals and services to whom I am indebted for their time, their interest and their assistance throughout the entire project, but I am particularly fortunate in my present phase of life to enjoy, not only the enduring support of my daughters, but also the inspiration, involvement and companionship of a very special friend. For these reasons, I dedicate this book to Céline, Linda and Irene.

Des Lavelle, Valentia Island

2018

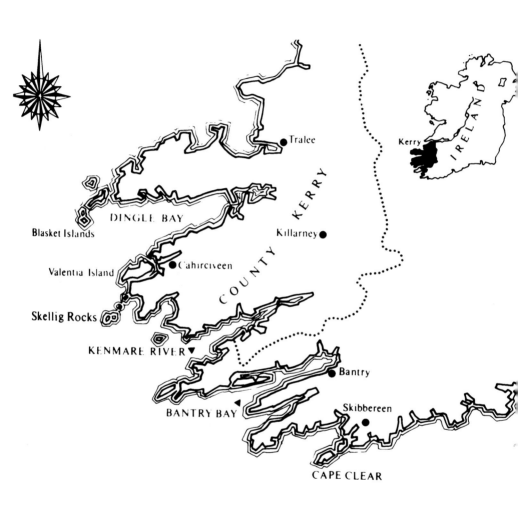

Skellig Islands location map.

CHAPTER ONE

LEGEND & HISTORY

'Like two mighty ships, sailing along majestically with every shred of canvas set'; such are the Skellig rocks – Skellig Michael and Small Skellig – located eight sea miles (14km) off Valentia Island on the Atlantic coast of Kerry. These great towering sea-crags, steeped as they are in history and legend, become daily more and more important in this age of bustle, pollution and all-consuming 'progress'. The archaeology of Skellig, the birdlife, the seals, the wide-open, timeless scenery – for one reason or another there is a balm for every soul on the Skelligs.

Visible from so many coastal vantage points between Dursey head in County Cork and Slea head in West Kerry, the Skellig Islands – Skellig Michael and Small Skellig – nonetheless seem to stand aloof, isolated and insulated from any mainland association.

This is but a latter-day impression. In any early age, a sea route was always an easier highway to traverse than the trackless mountains and boglands of the interior or the lengthy indentations of the local coast – Dingle bay, Ballinskelligs bay, Kenmare bay, Bantry bay...

Skellig and its environs were well travelled by such voyagers, local and international, throughout all eras, and it is hardly surprising that the wedge tomb at Cool East, Valentia Island, aligned ENE-WSW – as are many such megalithic monuments – in this instance, offers, from within the tomb, a tranquil scene of a well-known Skellig that is spiritually uplifting for any departing soul of any age or era.

The surprise is that more folk tales and legends do not abound.

A shipwreck around 1400BC, brought about by the magic of the Tuatha de Danann – a legendary pre-Celtic tribe – is one early reference to Skellig, when Milesius, leader of the early invasions of Ireland, lost two sons in the area:

Irr lost his life upon the western main;
Skellig's high cliffs the hero's bones contain.
In the same wreck Arranan too was lost,
Nor did his corpse e'er touch Ierne's coast.

Another legendary visitor was Daire Domhain – King of the World. He rested a while at the Skellig before his attack on the nearby coast and his legendary battle of a year and a day with Fionn Mac Cool's Fianna at Ventry.

Folklore also tells us that in the fifth century, Duagh, King of Munster, fled for his life to the isolation of Skellig when pursued by Aengus, King of Cashel. Likewise, we read that St Malachy, when driven from his monastery in Bangor, County Down, in the 12th century also sought the isolated Skellig haven.

Sanctuary, refuge, seclusion, afterlife – little wonder that Skellig offered itself as the ultimate outpost for the hermetical monks of the Early Christian era. In Egypt they had sought the desert fastness; in Ireland they sought the extreme headlands and the extreme islands. And there was no more extreme island than Skellig.

Yet, in its time, Skellig was neither heaven nor haven: In AD795, the first wave of Viking invaders from Scandinavia launched fierce attacks on the Irish coast, and the Skellig settlement did not escape their attentions for long. The early Irish manuscripts, the Annals of Innisfallen, Annals of Ulster and Annals of the Four Masters, contain only scant information on these raids, and there are no written sources in Scandinavia from the Viking period. However, we do know these sleek, clinker-built longships, with their high, graceful bow and shallow draught, were of advanced design in their age; some of them had a crew of forty, while others could be rowed or sailed at ten knots while carrying several hundred men.

In AD812, the Skellig monastery was sacked. Again in AD823, as reported in the Annals of Ulster and Annals of Innisfallen, the Vikings came and this time they took Etgal, Abbot of Skellig, and starved him to death. The years AD833 and AD839 saw further attacks when Turgesius, Sovereign of the Danes, swept through the area.

John Henry Newman, in his *Historical Sketches* (1917), gives a grim description of the Viking technique:

... the sea, instead of being a barrier, was the very element and condition of his victories and it carried him upon its bosom, up and down, with an ease and expedition which even in open country was impracticable. They ravaged far and wide at will, and no retaliation on them was possible, for these pirates, unlike their more civilised brethren

Some lines from one of the early Irish manuscripts. Note lines 3 and 4 – in Latin.

of Algiers or Greece, had not a yard of territory, a town, or a fort, no property but their vessels, no subjects but their crews. They were not allowed either to inherit or transmit the booty which these piratical expeditions collected … 'Never to sleep under a smoke-burnished roof, never to fill the cup over a cheerful hearth' was their boast and principle. If they drank, it was not for good company but by degrading extravagance, to rival the beasts of prey and blood in their wild brutality.

Patrick Foley in his book, *The Ancient and Present State of the Skelligs, Blasket Islands, etc*, (1903) adds:

They ran into land and set fire to villages and massacred the inhabitants. Whilst so engaged, their favourite sport was the tossing of infants on top of their lances to and from each other … Laws, religion and society they had no regard for. Both on sea and land their hands were always steeped in blood, murder and plunder. It was only when these pirates plundered and murdered each other that they finally collapsed.

But in spite of the attacks and the plundering, the monastic community of Skellig survived. In AD860 some rebuilding was done and recent studies of the long-ruined hermitage on the South Peak suggest that this too may have been a ninth-century addition. Other events of this era are noted in manuscripts: In the year AD885, Flan MacCallach, Abbot of Skellig, died. In AD950 the Annals of the Four Masters has the brief entry that Blathmac of Skellig passed away. Legend tells that in AD993 Viking Olav Trygvasson, who was later to become King of Norway and whose son, Olav II, was to become patron saint of Norway, was baptised by a Skellig hermit. The final report in this era, from the Annals of the Four Masters, dated AD1044, says simply: Aodh of Skellig died.

Such a conspicuous landmark as Skellig does not die silently; it has many lives and engenders tales, fact or fiction, from every era ... like the story of Ana Ní Áine – the old woman of Kenmare. Freely translated from Robin Jackson's *Scéalta ón mBlascaod*, it runs like this:

When I was a young woman my father had a pleasure boat and many strangers would come to our house to sail from place to place with him. One fine autumn day myself and another girl decided to accompany them to the Skellig; there was also a young priest in the boat with us.

We set out for Skellig, but before we reached the island a dreadful darkness approached from the West. My father wanted to put the boat around and head for home, but the others would not hear of this.

The dark cloud steadily approached with great gusts of wind. The priest looked towards it. 'There is some mystery in that cloud,' he said.

View from the tomb.

It was now bearing down on us until it was almost upon the boat, and then we could see that within the cloud was the spirit of a woman!

The priest jumped to his feet, put his confessional stole around his neck and took his book in his hands. He spoke to the woman and asked her what caused her unrest.

'I killed a person,' said the woman.

'That's not what damned you,' said the priest.

'I killed two people,' said the woman.

'It's not that either,' said the priest.

'I killed my own unbaptised child – whose father was a priest,' said the woman.

'That indeed is the cause of your damnation,' said the priest.

Then he began to read from his book and in a short moment the released spirit rose in a great flash and disappeared from sight.

We didn't continue to the Skellig that day; we returned home.

Maxwell's *A Book of Islands* (1945) leaves another such situation hanging in mid-air:

Everything was so peaceful that I climbed down to a concealed lighthouse on the island's outer flank to see if the night could be spent there. Meanwhile Tom pursued his archaeological study of the ruins.

The lighthouse men gave no encouragement. Nobody, they said, was allowed to stay without permission from Trinity House in Dublin. Nor would anybody in his senses want to stay there. The island was haunted and things often thumped on their own bolted door at night while the banshees wailed from the graveyard.

Surely, I suggested, this would be the shearwaters, but they replied with scorn that they knew all the birds as they had nothing else to study. It could be the monks with uneasy consciences, or it could be the poor souls whose lives they had been unable to save after a shipwreck a few years ago – or it could be something else...

Tom was sitting on the ground looking pale and shaken when I returned. Before I could speak, he said: 'For God's sake let's get off this island at once.' And then he added: 'Something nearly pushed me over the cliff when I was climbing to some nettles just below the oratory, and after I had got back to Christ's Saddle some force struck which threw me flat on my face.'

Coming from so powerful and fearless a man as Tom, this was extraordinary and, on top of what the lighthouse men had been saying, extremely sinister. Our descent to the boat was made with backward glances …

Monks, Vikings, priests, supernatural … as one gets to know the soul of Skellig it becomes easier to accept fact as fiction, and fiction as fact – and to be quite uninclined to probe the grey line between.

Early Christianity – carved in the solid stone of Skellig Michael.

CHAPTER TWO

PILGRIMAGE

The Skellig Michael that we know and visit today for entertainment and education was, for much of its known history, a place of pilgrimage, prayer and penance. Little wonder, then, that this island, like other similar high places, became dedicated to Michael, the Archangel, taking on the name by which it is known today: Sceilig Mhichíl.

It was here, says the legend, 'on this certain crag, surrounded on every side by the eddies of the great sea a distant a day's sail from the land', that St Michael appeared, together with others of the Heavenly Host, to help St Patrick banish the serpents and other evil things of Ireland into the sea. Likewise, with this early Christianity, came the founding of a monastery on Skellig – a small enclosure of stone huts and oratories which, though long since unoccupied, still stand firmly to this day near the island's northern pinnacle, some 182m above the sea.

And, as if this cliff-top site was not austere enough for the God-fearing monks of those times, an associated hermit's retreat on the island's 217m-high South Peak was the ultimate refinement in hardship and isolation!

From the South Peak, view of monastery site.

The founder of Skellig monastery is not named. Current tradition – without any supporting evidence – attributes it to one of two St Fionáns, and the influence of 'Fionán' is certainly strong in local place-names – Fionan's Well, Fionan's Bay, Fionan's Beach. Another possible, although seldom-mentioned, founder member of the monastic community is St Suibhne of Skellig, who is listed under 28th April in the Martyrology of Tallaght - a listing of saints and their Feast Days which was compiled at the monastery of Tallaght near Dublin at the end of the eighth century.

Nor is the exact date of the Skellig foundation known, but the style of building suggests the sixth century onwards. Other examples of such structures of similar dates can be found at many islands of Ireland's west coast. Most are but ruins, with perhaps only one significant stone or cross slab left. No manmade structure of this genre and this period stands in such perfect repair as the Skellig Michael monastery.

How these ascetic monks ever contrived to live on this 44 acre (18 hectares) crag is a mystery by today's standards. In summer, no doubt, they enjoyed seabirds, eggs and fish, but winter must have brought months of lean isolation. Against this, one can argue that the weather was better then, that sea travel was the norm, and that every soul on the coast was a master of the small, hide-covered boats of the period. But in any event, it seems unlikely that the Skellig community lived as well as their contemporary brethren on Church Island, in Valentia harbour, who – according to archaeological excavations of the midden there – enjoyed oats, barley, wheat, rye, cod, wrasse, seal, goat, pig, sheep, ox, pony, goose, duck, shag, cormorant and gannet!

Is one permitted to posit that the Skellig monks also were partial to gannet? This may explain the presence on Small Skellig of the remnants of a rectangular stone structure, high up on the south side and hidden from the view of passing boats: A gannet hunter's shelter of some bygone age, perhaps?

Unfortunately, Skellig Michael's cliff edge was too convenient a repository for domestic waste, and few artefacts have ever come to light to give us insight into the diet or the occupations of the Skellig monastic community. Restoration work and related excavations in the monastery area in recent years have yielded only some 110 finds. These include a bronze ring-pin (AD1000-1075), part of a decorated bone comb, a hone stone, an iron knife with a wooden handle and shards of mediaeval pottery. A fragment of cattle horn, dated to AD672-869, was found during the excavation at the Small Oratory terrace in 1986/87.

During the early lighthouse-building work in the nineteenth century, two archaeological finds were reported: 'Here we saw a small bronze figure of Our Saviour, about four inches [101mm] in height, found by the workmen in excavating. It was impossible to conceive anything more barbarous than this image, or nearer in resemblance to the rudest idol.' Another version says: 'A rude bronze crucifix with crown and kilted tunic, about four inches high [101mm], was found among the huts by the lighthouse workmen.' Fortunately, this item finally found its way to the Kerry County Museum in Tralee, but a second piece – 'A clay figure of the Virgin' – is no longer extant.

A stone water font, 197x114x127mm, which had been in the Large Oratory of Skellig monastery throughout all living memory, is currently retained by the Office of Public Works (OPW). It is thought to be late seventeenth or eighteenth century in date, and its presence on Skellig may be related to the pilgrimages of recent centuries.

One may dream that Skellig manuscripts similar to the Book of Kells or the other Irish Annals might exist and one day be discovered, but the harsh realities of the island must favour other conclusions; with minimal domestic equipment and few, if any, personal possessions other than the smock and cloak which they wore, membership of the Skellig monastery must have been a hard exercise in mere survival .

Welsh cleric and historian Giraldus Cambrensis reported at the end of the twelfth century that the Skellig community moved base to Ballins-kelligs 'on the continent', where the now-stabilised ruins of their medi-eval Augustinian abbey and its Saint Michael's church still stand today on the shores of Ballinskelligs bay. But the Skellig monastery did remain

The Southern climb begins.

occupied and in repair, and one particular church building in the monastic enclosure was extended in those Middle Ages. The ecclesiastical taxation of AD1300 refers to the 'Church of St. Michael's Rock' having a valuation of 20s (€1.27).

Early in the sixteenth century the Register of Primate Dowdall of Armagh lists Skellig Michael as one of the principal penitential stations for the performance of public penance. There is a record, too, of one sinner who was obliged to make a visit to the Skellig and other penitential stations as penance for murdering his own son.

Two centuries later, writers such as Friar O'Sullivan were still referring to Skellig Michael and to pilgrims arriving there from all over Ireland and Europe at Eastertime – not so much to visit the monastery, it would appear, but to perform the nerve-racking, difficult climb to follow the Stations of the Cross and finally kiss a standing stone slab overhanging the sea near the isolated hermitage of the Needle's Eye on the 217m-high South Peak of the island.

South peak Slab, lost in 1975.

Early writers report the climax of this climb in great detail, describing the pilgrim inching his way outwards, astride a narrow projecting spit of rock, reciting certain prayers and finally kissing the carved stone at the extremity before retiring to safety.

Notwithstanding recent restoration of the South Peak's oratory, associated terraces and stone-built stairway at the foot of the arduous 'chimney' access, the South Peak climb is best avoided by today's Skellig 'pilgrims' as access to this extremity is subject to a detailed advanced questionnaire and a prior written agreement with the OPW. In any event, the normal island visit is too brief – and, indeed, no longer is there any inscribed Standing Stone at the summit to kiss; it disappeared about 1977! It was not stolen, nor was it pushed over the precipice. More likely the wind and rain of a thousand years took their toll. And although amateur divers searched the depths of Blue Cove directly below this spot, no trace was ever found. Alas; another piece of Skellig history lost in a shattering, 217-metre tumble. Fortunate are we to have retained a 1976 photo of this precious monument.

Lady Chatterton, in *Rambles in the South of Ireland* (1839), recorded the following:

There is still living a gentleman who walked out to the eternity of this spit, and performing a regular pirouette, returned! However, the guides always encouraged the pilgrims by assuring them that no one was ever lost but an Englishman, who undertook the pilgrimage in order to ridicule the custom, and falling from the spit was drowned. From this circumstance a saying, much in use in this country, as applied to persons of ridiculously inordinate desires, had its origins. It runs thus:

"'More water," *arsa an Sasanach agus é á bhádhaid*h, or "More water", says the Englishman as he's drowning.' The tradition being that the unfortunate Sasanach found himself so long falling, as to call out for the rising of the sea in order to put an end to his tumble.

Charles Smith, in his *Ancient and Present State of the County of Kerry* (1756), shows a reproduction of 'The Skellig from the South West', but its gross inaccuracy proves clearly that this artist was never near the rock. His description of the monastery wells being 'a few yards above sea level', when in fact they are at a height of some 182m, leads to a similar conclusion.

The erroneous impression of Skellig Michael from Smith's *The Ancient and Present State of the County of Kerry* (1756).

In August 1779 one famous seaman, who certainly was no repentant pilgrim, almost came to grief upon the Skellig. *The French Archives* contain details from the Admiral's own pen: 'At 8.00p.m. Mizen Head lay astern, and with a fine breeze the squadron stood N.N.W. along the ironbound coast of Kerry. By noon we were five miles S.S.W. of Great Skellig.'

Here the fleet ran into a calm, and after some time the Admiral's flagship began to drift dangerously close to the Skellig – so close that her largest rowing boat had to be lowered to tow her clear. But the tale does not end there. The oarsmen were all Irishmen who had been 'pressed into service' against their wishes, and as soon as the flagship was out of danger – but still becalmed – they cut the tow rope and headed for Valentia at their best speed.

The flagship they had abandoned at the Skellig was the forty-two-gun Bonhomme Richard, and the Admiral they had outwitted was that master privateer, John Paul Jones.

Early in the nineteenth century, on the annual Feast of St Michael, the parish priest of Ballinskelligs, Fr Diarmuid O'Sullivan, used to visit Skellig Michael by boat to offer Mass on the island. Many people would travel with the priest on this pilgrimage, and the details of one particular visit, which was marred by a sudden gale, have been handed down in the poem '*Maidean Bhog, Áluinn I mBáidh Na Scealg*' by the Iveragh poet, Tomás Ruadh Ua Suilliobháin (1785–1848).

Maidean bhog, áluinn, i mBáidh Na Scealg,
Dul ag triall chum Aifrinn ghrádhmhair Dé,
D'éirigh an tsuail ró-mhór 'san bhfarraige,
Le fuadar fearthaine, d'arduigh gaoth.

Church Island cell, Valentia harbour. The midden revealed they enjoyed a varied diet, including gannet.

Do mhachtnuigh an chriú 'gus is umhal do chasadar,
Ag deanamh an chuain annuas chum Dairbhre,
'Nuair bhéic an fear stiúir, as mo shuan do phreabas-sa;
Do bhíos im' chodladh is dúisigheadh mé.

Cia chífeadh an bád ar bháidh an mhaidean úd,
Sáth' sé maide uirthe, is do b'árd í a léim,
'Nuair scaoileadar cnáib agus gárdaidhe rámha uirthe
Gach clár ag cnagadh, agus í ag rás mar philéar!
Do dheineamar í stiúradh ar chúrsa tarraingthe,
Sruthanna ag brúghadh le siubhal na hanairte,
Ní raibh luascadh ar an lín ó'n mBaoi go Daingean siar,
Go ndeachamair go Carraig Ghlas árd na Naomh.

Bhí Carraig Lomáin mar chráin ag screadadh rómhainn,
Ar tí sinn d'alpadh, le n-ár dtaoibh chlé;
Bealach na n-éigh do ghéim man tharbh romhainn,
Is dar ndóigh níor thaise do'n Ghearánaigh éigheamh
Céad moladh le hÍosa Críost nár cailleadh sinn!
Is ná fuairtheas sinn sínte I nduibheagán farraige,
Acht fanam' arís go dtigidh an chalma,
Agus racham dho'n charraig le congnamh Dé.

Do bhí an tAthair Diarmuid go dian ag agairt
Ar Rígh na nAingeal an chriú theacht soar,
Agus do chulathas shuas é i n-uachtar Pharathais.
'Nuair adubhairt an phaidir ós ár gcionn go léir.
Do ghlanamair poinnte Rinn' gil' Cathrach,
Bhí an Góilín shíos go mín, tais, calma,
Níor stadamair de'n scríb go ndeachamair dho'n Chalath.
Is d'ólamair fleagan 'dtig Sheain Mhic Aodha.

Bhí an fhuireann úd fuar tar éis uamhain na fairrge,
'Nuair do b'fhonn leis an sagart an chriú do théadh
Do thóg sé leis suas iad go cuan an mhaitheasa,
Ar bhruach an teaghlaigh úd Sheain Mhic Aodha.
D'fhanamair annsúd ag diúgadh an bharaille,
Mar a raibh fairsing de'n lionn le fonn d'a scaipeadh again;
Sinn ag faire ar gach uain go h-uair na maidne,
Agus an uamhain gur sheasaimh go fáinne an lae.

Is descair an bád do cháineadh, geallaim díbh,
Le grásta an Athair-Mhic tháinig soar,
Thug an fhuireann úd slán ó Bháidh na Scealg
An lá bhí anfadh árd 'san aer.
Ca bhfuil an t-árthach le fagh&áil do b'fhearra,
Do ghearrfadh casán tré lár na mara?
Dá dheascaibh sin táim-se fágaint barra
Ag an mbáidín greannta sin Sheain Uí Néill!

'A Fine, Soft Morning in Ballinskelligs Bay'
(Translated by Des Lavelle)

A morning sea of glass,
In Skelligs Bay,
Upon our way
To serve God's loving Mass.
A rise of swell,
And rain as well,
And storm soon came to pass.
Our prudent crewmen frowned,
But not for long.
Unwise to carry on,
And to Valentia Sound
We turned our yawl.
The helmsman's call
Enlivened all around.

Since early dawn arrived,
Our oar-blades light,
Our oarlocks tight,
Set every plank alive.
While bullet-speed she sped,
No ripple spread
By Beara, Dingle, or the Skelligside.

That roaring Lemon stone,
That hungry sow,
Would take us now.
The Puffin's Strait of Groans,
Gearánaigh gap,
A baited trap,
Bull-bellowing with foam.
To Jesus praises be.

Church Island in Valentia harbour, neighbours-in-time with Skellig.

We were not lost,
Nor paid the cost
Beneath the deepest sea.
So we shall 'tend
The tempest's end
Where e'er the haven be.
Dear Father Diarmuid prayed
To bring us through.
The angels too
Our words to God relayed.
Reen Point we passed,
And safe at last,
To Seán Mac Aodha's we strayed.

To drink a warming brew,
A flagon glass,
The night to pass,
A porter barrel too
To be consumed,
To lick our wounds
Until the day broke through.

Neill's boat was not to blame –
Nor oars nor men.
'Tis prudent when
The pathways through the main
Turn black and white,

Turn back; take flight;

And live to fight again.

Over the years the penitential nature of the early Skellig pilgrimages developed into something quite different. Patrick Foley puts it this way: 'Generally, in the latter days of these pilgrimages, the religious ceremonies were attended almost exclusively by girls and bachelors who were considered duly eligible for marriage. Of course, the idea was to spend Holy Week in fasting and praying. However, it transpired that many of the young "eligibles", instead of fasting and praying, visited the island with the intent of courting, dancing, drinking and enjoying themselves in other various amusements ...'

Finally, not only were the annual pilgrimages denounced from the altar but when the practice persisted the police got orders to clear the rock.

Possibly from these pilgrimages, possibly from the changes of the Gregorian calendar in 1782, or possibly because the abbot of the early monastery outranked the local bishop, a peculiar custom evolved – a tradition that the annual ecclesiastical period of Lent arrived later to Skellig than it did to the mainland, and consequently that marriage could still be contracted on the Skellig at times when this would be impossible on the mainland of Ireland. It is not known if anyone ever availed of this facility, but suggestions abounded in the annual 'Skellig Lists'. These were the anonymous and often highly defamatory poems of the era, once found throughout a wide swathe of the country – coastal and inland – from Dingle to Cork. They were a listing, and, to some extent, a lampooning of – not only the various local couples who were known to be 'going out' together – but often linking the most unlikely, lifelong spinsters and bachelors and suggesting that they should 'do the decent thing' and marry on Skellig while a few days remained before the onset of Lent!

Differing themes even existed from place to place: Valentia 'Lists' suggested that the participating couples might be mutually agreeable for the Skellig trip; in Killorglin, only forty miles away, the inference was that the gents would drag the ladies – screaming and kicking, perhaps – to a Skellig wedding. In any event, the Skellig Lists, arriving anonymously by post, were the big 'social media' posting of the day, to be pored over, copied, circulated, enjoyed or roundly condemned. Indeed, any 'young bloods' omitted from the List were often left feeling rather disgruntled!

And down in the cabin,
As Skellig draws near,
See Maggie so strongly caressed,
And Patsy McCann whispers,
'Shortly, my dear,
We'll hold our heads high like the rest!'
The Hegarty lad
From the Strand Street bohaun
Is there with his Mary tonight.
The Abbot of Skellig
Will wed them at dawn –
A wedding that cannot be white …

Of the many Skellig Lists retained in the Archives of the Department of

Irish Folklore, UCD, the List of 1922 from Lispole, in the Dingle Peninsula, is unique insofar as it deals – in humorous fashion – more with the nautical difficulties of sailing to Skellig than with the characteristics of the couples involved.

This Skellig group is depicted as departing from Minard harbour, but there was only one small boat – and that was already full …

Then up stepped Thomas Moran when he saw his craft was gone,
Saying comrades dear and maidens fair, I have for you a plan.
If you'll agree and follow me, we'll sail for Skellig too.
In a ship that's far more stately than a little mean canoe.
That barque lies over yonder we'll set afloat again,
And pack the holes up safely with bags of barley grain.
You need not be the least afraid; believe me when I say
She'll float as safe as Noah's Ark with you across the main.
Away we went with one consent to where Ruthickman lay,
And soon we had her floating on the waters of the bay.
The passengers, they went on deck, and all prepared to go.
'Twas then they found they had no sails,
Which filled their hearts with woe.
'Don't worry, boys,' said Moran, 'the ladies' shawls will do.'
He asked them and he got them – without a grumble too.
They tied them up along the masts, and when they caught the wind,
'Twas quick and soon they sailed away, and left Minard behind.

Skellig Lists such as these, some of them containing up to forty verses, were common throughout Munster for many years, but perhaps it is just as well that the custom died out a few generations before the millennium or Skellig and its would-be wedding hopefuls would surely feature in many a High Court libel action.

The letter that follows, received by a Cork printer in 1834, must be typical of the irate feelings of Skellig List victims.

Sir,

You are requested to take notice that I will hold you responsible for any liberties taken with the names of Mary Ellen Harris, Sarah Harris and Eliza Driscoll, they being members of my family, and having received intelligence of some person or persons wishing to expose them in the Skelligs Lists which are to come to and through your press, I am determined to indict all persons concerned if there is anything prejudicial to their person, interest or character in any manner.

Hugh Driscoll,
January 28, 1834

Onwards and upwards, steps and steps …

CHAPTER THREE

MONASTERY

Skellig and its monastery have changed hands, changed value and changed usage over the years: The lands of the mainland monastery at Ballinskelligs were disposed of in the sixteenth century, and included in the lease to Gyles Clinsher in 1578 was 'a small island called Skellig Michell …' Later, the island, which certainly was uninhabited by that time, passed to John Butler of Waterville for rental of 'two hawks and a quantity of puffin feathers yearly'. In fact, the 'quantity' of feathers amounted to some 114kg, which represented a considerable number of puffins!

About 1820, the body which is now the Commissioners of Irish Lights bought the island for the purpose of erecting a lighthouse. In 1871, shortly before the Office of Public Works (OPW) took over responsibility for the maintenance of the monastic site, Lord Dunraven produced the first detailed archaeological account of Skellig Michael. His depiction showed the whole monastic establishment rather as it still is today – a main enclosure of old stone dwellings and oratories, with some associated outbuildings, terraces and pathways throughout the island.

There is a long history of complaints about work carried out on Skellig. Certain renovations to the monastic site were attributed to the lighthouse workmen who, in 1838, 'built some objectionable modern walls'. Another report, of 1892, referring to repairs in the monastic site is more critical: 'We cannot conclude this account without protesting strongly against the way in which repairs are being carried out at Skellig Michael by the Board of Works. At the time of the visit of the Cambrian and Irish archaeologists, an ordinary mason was seen calmly tinkering away at the ruins, pulling down a bit here and building up a bit there in imitation of the old style of work, without any kind of superintendence whatever. The vandalism perpetrated some time ago by the same authorities, at Inishmurray is being repeated here with a vengeance'.

Environmental watchdogs were again growling – and perhaps not in vain – about some aspects of the repair, restoration, reconstruction and weedkiller-usage of the 1980s. Similarly, a UNESCO report of 2007 complained that conservation work had 'dramatically altered the appearance of the surviving ruins on the South Peak'. Likewise, local complaints were loud when the removal of accumulated soil near the Small Oratory was achieved by dumping it over the cliff and down into Blind Man's Cove.

In any event, for one's enjoyment today it is better to see Skellig – not in the light of nineteenth, twentieth, or twenty-first century operations – but in the deeper context of the Early Christian design, labour and accomplishment of this initial enormous feat.

Three ancient access stairways, cut and built into the rock faces, lead from sea level up to the monastery, 182m above the sea: The direct and steep eastern climb from Blind Man's Cove; the southern, part-mod-

Blindman's Cove
landing place and
(disused) eastern
stair.

ern, zigzag path from Cross Cove; and the picturesque northern path from Blue Cove, which joins the southern route at Christ's Saddle, 120m above the sea.

The eastern climb leads very steeply up the sheer face immediately above the landing at Blind Man's Cove. Having been overgrown and practically invisible for all living memory, restoration works in 2002/2003 have restored much of this stairway to its original glory and now, seen from the sea, it provides a striking feature that automatically leads the approaching eye up the cliff face to the monastic buildings high above on the island's skyline. It will, however, never be a public way as the lighthouse-builders of the 1820s, using explosives to blast out a roadway, demolished all the lower approaches to this climb.

Left: The final push to the monastery.
Opposite: Southern steps - the long descent from the monastery.

The northern stairway from Blue Cove to Christ's Saddle is also a picturesque scene that can be best-appreciated from the sea. This stair too has seen a long period of overgrowth and decay, but restorations of 2003 have again made a striking feature of this climb. The section approaching sea-level was enlarged by explosives during the lighthouse construction period of the 1820s. That it was used as a landing for lighthouse relief in some age is suggested by the story that potatoes once grew wild on this route – following the accidental rupture of a delivery bag – and an understandable reluctance or inability to scale the slopes again to salvage them!

Under present prevailing weather conditions, a small boat with a competent crew could use this north landing perhaps only ten days a year, so the fact that the monks of old undertook the giant task of constructing a stairway to this currently-inhospitable cove is a good argument that the weather conditions then were far better than today.

This northern 'bare rock' landing is not a commercial passenger option; it never was. Likewise, its related northern stairway is not a public area today. Little wonder this; the looming, overhanging cliff is subject to frequent rockfalls – one such notable event coinciding with an earthquake of Magnitude 4 that occurred off the Mayo coast on 6th June 2012.

The south landing, exposed to the SE/SW, was useful in its time for small, easily-managed boats. It consists of steps carved into the solid rock from sea level to roadway – thereafter linking with the conspicuous Southern Climb. No doubt, this original work of the monastic period may well have been embellished by the lighthouse builders of the 1820s. There is some mystery nearby too: Carved into the rock face under today's helicopter pad are fourteen steps which are virtually inaccessible, stopping short at both ends and leading neither to the sea nor to the higher levels!

Another technical puzzle is this: how, and where (without the benefit and convenience of the modern road) did the monks keep their boats safely out of reach of the sea? Today, a considerable amount of manhandling or engineering would be involved! However, if one argues that the weather was better in the Early Christian era, perhaps they did not have to lift their boats so far to find safety?

To reach the monastery today, one follows the lighthouse road from the landing point at Blind Man's Cove to a junction just beyond Cross Cove where the real ascent to the monastery begins via the old Southern stairway of some 600 steps.

Access to the monastery enclosure is via a low archway into the Monks' Garden followed by a low tunnel in the main retaining wall and upon emerging within the shelter of this enclosure – some 100m x30m – one finds the old stone dwellings and oratories huddled close together at various levels, almost as perfect as when first built.

'The scene is one so solemn and so sad,' says Lord Dunraven, 'that none should enter here but the pilgrim and the penitent. The sense of solitude, the vast heaven above and the sublime monotonous motion of the sea beneath would oppress the spirit, were not that spirit brought into harmony …'

Six corbelled, beehive-shaped huts and two boat-shaped oratories, many stone crosses and slabs, some graves, two 'wells' – said to 'become dry in case of cursing, swearing or blasphemy' – and the ruin of a medieval church occupy the site. Tradition tells that there is also a deep subterranean tunnel leading away from the monastic site, but although there are

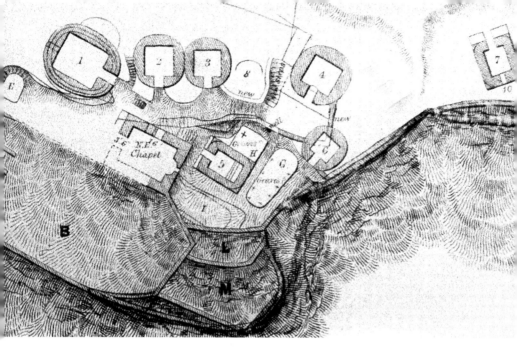

Above: A sketch plan of the monastery complex by Lord Dunraven. This plan is based on the plan from Dunraven's *Notes on Irish Architecture* (1875), but the author has added additional detail and used a different code for the dwellings. In the 1980s conspicuous alterations included: the removal of the steps between A and B and the erection of a wall there; the rerouting of the steps between D and E; the clearing and reconstruction of the terrace levels in front of A, B, C, D, E; the reconstruction of the small oratory.

Left: An engraving from *Lord Dunraven's Notes on Irish Architecture* (1875). This gives a rather elaborate and misleading impression of the site. This beautiful cross had fallen, broken in two and become completely overgrown until its rediscovery in 1974.

two features in the enclosure which could be associated with this tale, there is no clear evidence of any such tunnel today.

MONASTIC CELLS:

All the monastic buildings have undergone some degree of restoration/repair since such works began in 1978. If such repairs are not evident to the casual observer, it is a testimony of the expertise of the local OPW workforce who have invisibly blended the old and the new.

The monastery cells are rectangular in plan at floor level and take on a circular shape as the corbelling progresses upwards. We take them in the order in which one meets them.

Skellig Michael's monastic site prior to the restoration of the fallen retaining wall (right foreground).

Above: Cells and memorials.
Below: Cells and shadows.

Above: Teetering on the brink, the Small Oratory sits precariously on a man-made buttress.

Below: Detail from the roof of Cell A. It is thought that the protruding stones here used as anchorages to secure protective sods or thatch.

CELL A

Cell A has a floor area of 4.5m x 3.8m and a height of 5m. The internal walls are almost straight to a height of 1.5m before the dome begins to narrow, and all around the interior of the walls, at about 2.5m, are protruding stone pegs, which may have supported a wooden upstairs floor. The window high up on the west wall would have given light at this level. On the exterior of the hut more stone pegs protrude and these may have been anchorages for protective sods or thatch. The door is 1.2m x 0.8m and the walls are 1.8m thick.

Below: The monastery entrance.
Opposite top: The view through an oratory window.
Opposite bottom: The cross slab in the enclosure.

CELL B

Cell B is 2.7m x 2.7m x 3m high. There are two cupboard recesses in the internal walls, but no windows or protruding pegs inside or out. The door is 1.3m x 0.6m and the walls are 1.06m thick at the door.

CELL C

Cell C is 2.7m x 2.6m x 3.4m. It is quite like Cell B, being without windows or protruding stones. The door is also of a similar size.

CELL D

Cell D is now only a ruin; it may have been circular in plan originally. Its collapse is not of recent times.

CELL E

Cell E is very similar to Cell A. It also has the internal stone pegs on the walls. The floor, which is very well laid, is 3.6m x 3.5m and the height is 3.9m. The door is 1.4m x 0.9m and the walls are 1.2m thick.

Heading back down.

CELL F

It is thought that the roof of this cell collapsed between 1871 and 1891, and that the dome was reconstructed inaccurately, some 0.9m less than originally. This cell is now 2.5m x 2.7m x 3m. There are three cupboard recesses in the internal walls and again there are internal stone pegs. The door is 1.2m x 0.6m and the walls are 1.1m thick at the door.

LARGE ORATORY

This building is boat-shaped with a door in the western wall. Its measurements are 3.6m x 2.4m x 3m. The stone altar that occupied the eastern wall was completely removed during the renovations of 1990 – causing some dismay to those who argued that such works – (of the 19th century lighthouse builders) – were of archaeological significance too.

SMALL ORATORY

Some distance away from the group, the Small Oratory is located on a substantial artificial terrace that has undergone extensive (underground) reinforcement in recent years . It is 2.4m x 1.8m x 2.4m and a window, 0.6m x 0.3m, occupies the northeastern wall. The door is only 0.9m x 0.5m and the walls are 1m thick. .

MEDIEVAL CHURCH

The enclosure's medieval church is quite ruined, but its eastern gable still stands. As distinct from the other buildings of the monastery, the construction of this medieval church involved the use of some imported stone

The uninterrupted view from the small oratory on Skellig Michael across to Small Skellig.

– identified as coming from Reenadrolaun Point on Valentia Island – a feat of transport and labour which is almost unbelievable. The church's remaining walls and its eastern gable have undergone much conspicuous restoration in recent years and the East window's heavenly view of Small Skellig still lives on.

Archaeological excavations unearthed some eight human burials, dated 10th/13th centuries, close outside this gable – adult males of average stature 5'6" (170.6cm) and children aged between 9-11 years. Within the church, modern restoration is noted in the form of a new replica gravestone where rest the Callaghan lighthouse children of 1868. A new slab of Valentia slate replaces the original, dated 1871 which was long since broken. That original slab has found a new home in the Skellig Experience Visitor Centre on Valentia.

Restoration work.

Danger – Right turn! Safety and caution are paramount on the descent too!

All quiet at Skellig landing.

CHAPTER FOUR

SEA JOURNEY

The modern Skellig 'pilgrim' might well assume that all the ancient problems of access to the island have been eliminated in this age of sturdy, glassfibre, diesel-engined boats; but he would be wrong! True, the modern Skellig passenger boat is far removed from the hide-covered craft of old, and even from the modified fishing boat of yesteryear. True also, it would be quite possible nowadays to beat a reasonable passage to Skellig through most weather – fog, calm or Force 5 wind – but irrespective of the mode, comfort, difficulty or ease of the sea journey from the mainland, the sea conditions immediately around Skellig's only landing place at Blindman's Cove still dictate access to the island.

Of course, it was never necessary to travel all the way to Skellig to assess the landing conditions there; local mainland boatmen of old have had a yardstick closer to home that gave them a very accurate appraisal of the possibilities. A Valentia man, for instance, could look at the 'Holy Ground' foreshore in nearby Lough Kay and decide on that observation if a Skellig landing wouild be feasible. A Derrynane man might view 'The

Pigs' rocks outside his own harbour and base his decision on the conditions there. This was something that inevitably baffled the old-time visitor: On what appeared to be a perfect summer's day, no boatman would take a Skellig landing party to sea!

These yardsticks may still be accurate today, but nowadays the variety and detail of online weather forecasts deliver total 'Skellig' information to all at the click of a button on phone or tablet; not just the sun, wind and rain, but also more vital information, like the height, direction and wave-to-wave period of the surrounding Atlantic swell. Experience now tells that – while one might master local wind and wave on the passage – if the period between each swell is 12 seconds or more, and if it is coming from the northwest or the south, the prudent skipper may opt to remain in port rather than attempt a Skellig landing. Add but another notch or two to this weather data, and Skellig shall again become an inaccessible, mystery-place beyond the surf and the spray.

Calm approach.

So the visitor must wait for tomorrow – or the day after... And ponder that this inaccessibility – in an age when we have access to the moon – is all part of the powerful magnetism of Skellig, the enhanced attraction of the unattainable!

In winter, such seafaring is out of the question. Even a whole week without wind in the period November to March – an unlikely occurrence at best – would hardly be sufficient to calm the ocean around Skellig. During this season, Skellig cliffs are sea-lashed from every side. Great long swells, which may have travelled 2,000km from some distant depression, mingle with local gales to create a terrible fury in which the Skellig landing is scarcely visible. Winter wave crests will break 10m high over the pier and reach 45m up along the lighthouse road, as evidenced in February 1988 when some of the OPW workmen's cabins – together with sections of the masonry wall which protected them and the roadway on which they stood – were wrecked by storm waves. The receding turmoils of wave-troughs such as these expose the ragged seaweed stumps, sponges and anemones on rock faces which are normally 10m below the mean surface. And this is the sheltered side of the island!

From March onwards, conditions can be expected to improve, and on fine summer days, boats from Valentia, Portmagee, Ballinskelligs and Derrynane offer a passenger service for visitors to Skellig.

The traveller of 150 years ago could hire a rowing boat and four oarsmen exclusively for a Skellig trip for 25s (€1.59) a day. Such an outing – a full, tiring day in any sense – was not for everyone, and even as late as the 1960s a Skellig trip was quite a rarity. By 1970, tourism demands prompted one fishing boat or two to 'double up' as Skellig passenger boats on a more frequent basis; in 1973 the visitor had a choice of five boats –

Des Lavelle at the wheel. (Photo: Hartmut Krinitz.)

at a fare of £3 (€3.81) per person. And by the 1990s, the team of Skellig wardens employed by the Office of Public Works (OPW) since 1987, were hard-pressed to manage the large numbers of visitors, as ten boats from four harbours ran a busy Skellig service at £15 (€19) per person.

But for the moment, let's experience a leisurely Skellig trip from the hazy days of 1975.

It is 10.45am on a fine summer's morning at Knightstown harbour, Valentia Island. The Shannon/Fastnet weather forecast is good – 'South-west, Force 2/3; Visibility 25 miles (41km); 1033 millibars; Steady', and a glance at the still waters at the 'Holy Ground' indicates a good day for a Skellig visit. One of the local boats, the *Beal Bocht*, is preparing to make the trip. Half a dozen passengers – all foreign visitors – step on board with well packed lunch boxes and a selection of sweaters and rain coats – 'just in case'!

'Cast off.' We have a brief stop at nearby Renard Point pier to pick up two more passengers, and then we set off southwards through the five-mile corridor of Valentia harbour. On either hand, pebble beaches slope upwards to green field, ochre bogland and blue mountain. Local landmarks are noted and discussed – the conspicuous Victorian terraces of the now-closed Western Union transatlantic telegraph cable station, and further on, the long-ruined 'Revenue' building that housed Valentia's original weather station in 1868.

Kindred spirits on board recognise one another across barriers of language, race and age in the spontaneous camaraderie of a shared shipboard adventure. Binoculars are compared with interest and the merits of German, Japanese and Russian brand-names are extolled. At least there is consensus on one point: 7x50mm is the most suitable for boat-work where motion must be considered. Cameras, similarly, are much in evidence, from the Hasselblad to the Box Brownie. They may vary in quality and operation, but the end products are very similar: memories of a certain summer's day.

Black guillemots – red-legged, black-beaked, and really as much white as black in appearance – occupy our attention. They spend their lives, summer and winter, here in the sheltered shallows of the harbour and seldom venture out to the open sea. Yet, of all the seabirds, their nests are the most secluded.

Stiff-legged along the water's edge, each guarding a mile territory, stand the herons. Grey, hump-backed and sombre – but ever alert – they await low water to go fishing; and if the wake of our passing boat slops about their knees, it bothers them not..

Valentia bridge and Portmagee village are reached and the tiny monas-

Map showing the lie of the land on Skellig Michael.

tic island of Illaunloughan is noted in passing and soon left behind. Our channel widens; we are in Foilhommarum bay. This small, stony beach and its surrounding cliffs brought world renown to Valentia island in 1866, being the landing point of that first successful trans-Atlantic telegraph cable linking Ireland – and Europe – to Canada and the United States. Valentia's Bray Head, one of the western extremities of the Irish coast, now looms high on our starboard hand. The conspicuous tower on its extremity is also of interest – being one of the many 'Martello' lookout posts built by the British authorities of the early 1800s to warn in the event of an anticipated invasion by the French fleets of Napoleon. Here, we are entertained by common terns from the colony on nearby islands, dangling on fragile wings and performing their exquisite fishing dive – which our eyes view as a floppy splash! On the port hand, we clear Long Island, and at last we catch our first glimpse of Skellig, directly ahead and some eight nautical miles (12km) away. This is the transition point between harbour and ocean and we feel the first gentle touch of the Atlantic in one of her kinder moods. Our course is 225° (C); speed 7.5 knots; destination: Skellig Michael – 51° 46' 20" N, 10° 32' 58" W; ETA: 12.55pm, local time!

The vast panorama of the open sea expands around us. To the north lie the Blasket Islands and the Tearaght lighthouse some 15 nautical miles (27km) away, a wide, empty horizon occupies the west, the two Skelligs are on our stem to the southwest and Puffin Island – rich bird sanctuary of the Irish Wildbird Conservancy – fills our southern view. Astern, we view the Old Devonian sandstone cliffs of Kerry's Macgillycuddy Reeks standing tall and ever ready to do battle with the Atlantic Ocean – futile though this may be!

Out here, we meet the oceanic seabirds: guillemots, puffins, razorbills, fulmars – swimming, flying, diving and making a living in their various ways. An alarmed puffin surfaces too near the boat; Its panic-stricken escape – half flying half swimming – amuses everyone. To the west, flocks of noisy kittiwakes vigorously work a shoal of sprat, and farther on, the black, triangular dorsal fin of a basking shark protrudes almost 1m above the surface of the sea. This remarkable giant – which may be as long as our boat – wanders slowly about the seasonal tidal streams, its awesome, gaping, white mouth doing nothing more sinister than collecting micro-scopic plankton! If we take the boat too near, the shark simply slides down out of sight for a few moments and returns lazily to its meal of surface plankton when all is clear. If curious divers wish to sneak up close to get the photo-of-the-day, the shark hardly cares!

Dolphins! Over there! The common dolphin is ready for interaction and fun. In pods of a dozen or many hundreds they range the ocean,

Above: Bottle-nosed dolphin at Small Skellig.
Below: Common dolphins along the way.

and it's an exciting event when they decide to play – following the boat, accompanying it, racing it, jumping over the bow wave, surfing on the wake, always confident that they can beat our best speed at their leisure! This is a photo-fest – if you are quick on the trigger.

The first gannet – a reconnaissance outrider from the Small Skellig colony – flies overhead on a ceremonial circuit of inspection. It is followed by others and still more, and as we approach the island a thousand gannets are in the air around us. Further thousands occupy every visible ledge on Small Skellig, and as many more are plummeting like guided missiles into a fish shoal near the shallow reef on the northern side of the island. Where could you better this incredible sight? Possibly one place in the world! Only St Kilda in the Outer Hebrides can boast more gannets than Small Skellig's 23,000 pairs.

'*Regardez le phoque!*' '*Kijk naar de zeehonden!*' 'Seals! Seals! There on the rocks!' Cameras are trained and focussed and shot – and ultimately re-loaded with feverish haste as ten or a dozen seals maintain their obliging photogenic poses...

Eventually Skellig Michael, our final goal, looms high above us, solid, massive, awe-inspiring, its sheer cliffs leading all the way to heaven. We throttle back and slip alongside the tiny pier in Blindman's Cove where one of the lighthouse men is waiting to lend a hand. Our lines are made fast. The engine is stopped. It is 12.55pm. A modern pilgrimage to Skellig has begun!

We have much to do, much to admire, and the roadway leads us on: Two hundred yards from the pier, the man-derrick, with red-leaded hand-winch and giant pitch-pine spar - standard equipment of every island lighthouse - stands ever ready to transfer lighthouse men between

Blindman's Cove landing place – with Skellig's (disused)
Eastern stair leading upwards to the skyline and
the monastery.

Boatmen chatting in Blue Cove.

boat and island if sea swells rule out a pier landing.

Cross Cove is next on our way, the kittiwake-clamour of its citizens reverberating a hundred-fold throughout this rocky sound-chamber. Here, another derrick, diesel-powered and judiciously installed on the roadside clifftop to hoist lighthouse cargo - coal by the ton, paraffin oil by the barrel, lighthouse equipment by the crate - from the relief ship's small workboat that can pull right into the cove below in appropriate sea conditions.

A stairway in stone soon faces us - a climb to the monastic site to wander and wonder in personal silence in its awe-inspiring atmosphere, a further testing climb to the 714-ft (217m) South Peak, to note the ruins of a small rectangular structure that once was the home of Skellig's most extreme hermit, a pause to admire the hand carved cisterns that gathered rainwater for his needs, and, ultimately to view - with timidity and respect - the pinnacle's standing stone slab on its protruding spit that has been the climax of many an age-old penetential pilgrimage to this island..

No landing at Skellig today;
resident staff stand well back.

Later, we must visit Skellig lighthouse – thrown open to all visiting friends. Here we can admire its magnificent lens of 1909 and its polished brass controls. If we are lucky, we may enjoy a cup of lighthouse tea, always special – perhaps because of the ambience, perhaps because it is made with rainwater! Then, thus fortified, set out again to undertake the next climb up the steep, winding road to the silence and tranquility of the old North Station lighthouse – disused since 1870 and quite ruined now.

One thing is certain: On this fine day in The Year of the Lord, 1975, nobody will dream of leaving this magical island until the evening is well advanced!

The Skellig trip of today is not quite like this. Notwithstanding the fact that every tourism body, from Failte Ireland, Discover Ireland and the Wild Atlantic Way, to the smallest local tourist office, sells Skellig in a thousand ways, modern-day concerns put apparent disincentives in the way of the aspiring Skellig visitor...

It is worth noting the details – because they are extreme: The OPW'S Safe Access Guide leaflet, which is lavished on every tourist office and visitor service desk, carries stark warnings about the Skellig trip.

'Transferring between a boat and the landing pier can be hazardous… there is risk of serious injury or death'.

'The lighthouse road and access routes are exposed to loose overhead rock'.

'The access route includes steep uneven steps with unprotected edges'.

'Steps can be slippery when wet'.

'The terrain includes sheer cliffs; please stay on the designated access route'.

'Straying from the access route involves a high risk of fall or tumble'.

Likewise, the OPW'S stainless-steel notice boards mounted prominently at the mainland departure piers add further highlighted bullets:

WARNING Beware of falling rocks.

WARNING Sheer drop with no edge protection.

WARNING Steps slippery when wet.

'Danger' Skellig noticeboard.

WARNING Steep gradient on steps.

WARNING Uneven steps.

Again, the OPW'S specially-commissioned Skellig Safety Film, conspic-uous on-line, and running in an endless loop in The Skellig Experience Visitor Centre since 2016, augments the warnings of brochure and notice board with urgent voice-over and video close-ups of many stone steps and many ascending and decending boots!

And if all this is still not enough to dampen enthusiasm, the intrepid Skellig visitor shall see and hear all the warnings again upon reaching the island!

In effect, no visitor shall mount a step of a Skellig stair in ignorance of the terrain.

OPW safety talk.

An aerial view of Skellig from the east.

But there are grounds for the OPW'S concentration on safety: As well as some minor mishaps, involving lifeboat and helicopter evacuation, three (unrelated) visitor fatalities have occurred on Skellig in modern decades. Litigation ensued in two of these. Furthermore, an OPW-commissioned Skellig Safety Review of 2010 pointed clearly to the need for Safety Warnings in every medium.

The daily tempo of a modern Skellig visit also moves at a different pace to that of old: Your trip begins at an earlier hour. When you step on board, your skipper will give you a briefing on safety aspects and lifejacket usage – and point out that there is no obligation to wear these bulky devices except in an emergency. Your boat, once it clears the harbour, is now travelling outbound at some fourteen knots – or possibly more – if a nor'westerly breeze offers its help. The common terns of yester-year no longer entertain us at the harbour mouth; they have followed their food source to other waters. Common dolphins still frolic as of old – still

Left: Colourful, rare summer visitors.
Below: Small Skellig; sunrise erupting.

easily outdoing our now-increased speed. Bottle-nosed dolphins – generally more reserved in their behaviour – can sometimes surprise us with their aerial acrobatics, and sightings of minke – and other – whales, newcomers to the region in recent years, provide real excitement on occasion.

Where Skellig passengers of old were exposed to all the elements, sheltered decks, 'dodgers' and related refinements in the Skellig fleet now offer protection from sun, rain, wind and spray. Modern, onboard, marine toilets are a particular bonus, as this basic facility is not available on Skellig!

At Skellig itself, there are changes of tempo too: Boats at the landing no longer tie-up for a day or an hour. Brisk traffic – arriving or departing – means that each boat must move out from the jetty and give access to the fourteen other authorised vessels that may be in line for a slot to land or pick up passengers. But an agreed marine operation is in evidence here: Boatmen space their arrivals to minimise congestion at the Safety talk at the foot of the monastic stairway and to optimise the visitors' time at the historical discourse in the monastic enclosure.

Today's visiting time on Skellig Michael does not include the lazy summer evenings of yore; a two-and-a-half hour visit is now the norm. It may be less if the weather threatens. However – on especially calm days – you may be treated to a round tour of the island to view the two lighthouses and the old North landing before you head for home.

But the physical solitude of old is scarcely diminished. Only one hundred and eighty visitors a day share the island – between 10am and 4pm – and, whatever the motivation for this visit, Skellig will not disappoint. This is a place for the inner soul, irrespective of the external pressures, cares and liabilities of the modern day.

Lighthouse roadway.

CHAPTER FIVE

LIGHTHOUSE

Prior to 1820 there was no lighthouse between Cape Clear, County Cork, and Loop Head, on the River Shannon – some 179km, as the gull flies, of Ireland's fiercest coast. In 1820, on the request of Sir Maurice FitzGerald, Knight of Kerry, approval was granted for a lighthouse on Skellig Michael. The Corporation for Preserving and Improving the Port of Dublin – predecessors of today's Commissioners of Irish Lights – bought the island from Butler of Waterville for the sum of £780 (€990), and engineer George Halpin was given a formidable construction task:

To distinguish Skellig Michael from Loop Head or Cape Clear, and to ensure a wide arc of visibility, the plan called for two lighthouses on Skellig Michael – one at 53m above sea level near Seal Cove, and the other at twice that elevation on the island's western extremity. It also called for some 2km of approach road to be built – or blasted out of the solid rock – from one end of the island to the other and clinging to the cliff face every step of the way.

Desirable though the project was, some writers of the period were greatly alarmed by one aspect of the construction work: In his sale, Butler had stipulated that the monastery buildings be carefully preserved, but it transpired that the road-builders and lighthouse-builders had been living in some of the monastery cells and using others for storing explosives. It is not clear how much the monastery suffered in this period, but other setbacks were also noted:

In December 1821, the sloop, *John Francis*, belonging to contractor, Mr Hill, was burned off Portmagee while ferrying materials for the Skellig lighthouse construction.

Mr Hill sought compensation, but the Board declined to pay! On 16 November 1825, one of the Skellig workmen, Peter Kane of Portmagee, was killed in a rock-blasting operation. His widow submitted a petition to the Board in the following February – and was awarded a pension of £6 per annum for herself and £3 per annum for each of her children

Clinging to the cliff face – the modern lighthouse and the long-ruined old North Station (foreground).

under age sixteen.

However, by 1826, at a cost of £45,721 (€58,054), the two lighthouses were established, each showing a steady light from Argand oil lamps and parabolic reflectors, and each having two semi-detached houses close by, where the keepers and their wives and families resided for long periods of duty. Writing in 1837, Samuel Lewis reported: 'The erection of the lighthouses has been a means of preventing much loss of life and property. Scarcely a winter previously elapsed without frequent and fatal shipwrecks ...'

One of the fatal Skellig shipwrecks to be recorded was the wreck of the Lady Nelson. Northbound from Oporto with a cargo of wine and fruit, she struck the Skellig and went to pieces with the loss of all but three lives. Lady Chatterton wrote of the case in 1839:

The mate had warned the captain during the evening of his proximity to this dangerous rock; but the captain, who was drunken and jealous (his wife having seconded the representations of the mate), refused to put the vessel about and in a couple of hours she struck.

The mate and three hands saved themselves upon a part of the wreck, which was drifting about for two or three days, during which time they subsisted on the oranges and other fruit which, when the ship went to pieces, covered the sea around them. The mate, who was an excellent swimmer, procured these oranges by plunging off the spar and bringing them to his companions. On the third day, one man became delirious; saying that he should go ashore to dine, he threw himself off the spar and sank.

Shortly afterwards the survivors were picked up by a fishing boat belonging to Dingle, which had come out looking for a wreck. The crew consisted of a father and his four sons, and had two pipes of wine in tow when they perceived the sufferers; finding their progress impeded by the casks and that the tide was sweeping the seamen into the breakers, where they must have been dashed to pieces, the old man nobly cut the towline, abandoning what must have been a fortune to his family, and by great exertion picked the men up, just when the delay of a second would have caused their destruction.

The Lady Nelson port is still famous in Kerry, and a glass of it is sometimes offered as a 'bon bouche'.

What was life like at the Skellig lighthouses in those pioneer days? Perhaps there were good times, but it is generally the hardship that is most remembered. Hugh Redmond of Wexford, one of the first Skellig lighthouse crew, lost both his sons and his nephew over the cliffs. John Sloane, writing in 1873, recorded in some detail that another of the early Skellig lighthouse men arrived there – and departed – in very unhappy circumstances indeed. Michael Wishart had been principal keeper on the Tuskar Rock lighthouse in 1820 when he and his assistant, Charles Hunter, became involved in a substantial smuggling enterprise: '... A large cask and several small kegs of brandy up to 84 proof ... and other excisable commodities.' Not only were they storing the goods on the Tuskar, but they made the mistake of sampling them so heavily that they were unable to light the lantern, which, of course, provoked deep inquiry. 'I gained the tower, and on entering it, found Hunter dead drunk on his back and Wishart in the same state on his side, they having Tapped the Admiral.'

On 23 October 1821, Michael Wishart was demoted from his post

Only on a round-tour of the island can one appreciate the lighthouse's strategic location fifty metres above the sea.

of principal at Tuskar and later sent to Skellig as assistant, where he was killed when he fell over the cliff while cutting grass for his cow!

It must have taken considerable labour to land a cow on Skellig – presumably by means of a manual cargo derrick at Cross Cove. It also called for considerable imagination as to how a cow might access grazing of any sort there! But it is easy to visualise such an accident on the steep rocky slopes of Skellig. Even a century later, Thomas Mason wrote: 'The lighthouse keepers have a couple of goats which are generally located in some almost inaccessible position at milking time. With bated breath I have watched the men retrieve these perverse animals … there is no place in the scheme of nature for a giddy goat …'

Lighthouse reconstruction, 1966.

It was 1862 before wooden partitions were added to some of the Skellig lighthouse bedrooms 'to give more privacy', but the inter-family privacy between the two Skellig lighthouses must also have been in some question, because in April 1865 the principal keeper of the lower lighthouse was dismissed for having 'cruelly beaten up' the principal keeper of the upper station!

In or about 1870, Thomas McKenna of Crookhaven was dismissed from his post at Skellig lighthouse for being absent from duty when the Commissioners made a surprise visit. But where had he been? McKenna had gone exploring an underground tunnel in the monastery site, but he ran into difficulty and was unable to get out. Eventually, his plight was discovered and one of his companions also entered the tunnel with a rope and brought McKenna to safety – but not before the Commissioners had appeared on the scene, made their feelings known and ordered that the entrance to the tunnel be closed … Was this the underground tunnel of the earlier legend?

Another place with a story, which is lost today because of rockfall-related closure in the area, is Eliza's Corner – a sheltered spot on the roadway between the two lighthouses, so named by Portmagee tradesmen who were working on the rock some 150 years ago. Eliza Callaghan, after whom the place was called, was a young woman who used to sit out at this corner for hours on end, knitting in the sunshine. But was she a lighthouse daughter, much admired by the Portmagee men, or was she the mourning mother of the two children, Patrick and William Callaghan, who died in 1868 and 1869, aged two and three years, and are buried in the medieval church ruin in the monastery? Nobody knows...

One sad note, which is recorded in the minutes of the Lighthouse

A lighthouse helicopter service, introduced in 1969, made lighthouse life and management much easier than earlier boat-dependant operations.

Board on 3 April 1869, is a letter from W. Callaghan, principal keeper of the lower Skellig lighthouse, 'requesting removal to another station, stating that he had buried two of his children on the island and that another was lying ill …' The request was noted by the inspector, but was not immediately carried out. Indeed, it must have been easy to die on Skellig in those days. In 1851 Skellig visitor John Windele also records a conversation with lighthouse man Rooney, who had 'lost a son by being clifted' at Seal Cove.

That other families with young children occupied Skellig about 1889 is also known because the late Mrs O'Sullivan (1869–1963) of Portmagee, formerly Miss Joanie Cahill, often recalled spending three years of her youth on Skellig Michael as a teacher to the lighthouse children.

The final chapter in Skellig families was completed when James Martin King, second son of Thomas and Mary King, was the last child to be born on Skellig on 30 October 1897.

However distant these parishioners, they were not exactly forgotten by the mainland Church – politically, at least. In 1889 the Lighthouse Board received a communication from the parish priest of Cahersiveen, claiming that – in the interest of the Roman Catholic Church – the Skellig lighthouse-keepers, who, since 1880, had been appointed 'caretakers' of the Skellig monuments, should 'be of the Faith', and requesting that the present Protestant keepers be replaced. The Board ordered that 'the reverend gentleman be informed that they cannot accede to this request, but that every care is taken of the monuments'!

Finally, about 1900, a decision was taken to move the lighthouse men's families to the mainland, and a block of eight dwelling houses (for Skellig and Inishtearaght families), was built on Valentia by Mr W.H. Jones

Over Seal Cove, Skellig.

of Dunmanway at a total cost of £7,570 (€9,612). Thus, Knightstown village took over from Portmagee, which had been the Skellig shore base since 1820.

This is not to say that there was now some permanence of residence for the lighthouse men and their families. In fact, the uprooting and many trans-Ireland gyrations continued – of which the various appointments of Thomas King, mentioned in an earlier paragraph, are typical:

1890, Inishtearaght, (Kerry)

1893, Ballycotton, (Cork)

1896, Skellig, (Kerry)

1899, Fanad Head, (Donegal)

1900, Inishtearaght, (Kerry)

1902, Rockabill, (Dublin)

1902, Bailey, (Dublin)

1906, Rockabill, (Dublin)

1908, Ballycotton, (Cork)

1912, Kinsale, (Cork)

1914, South Aran, (Galway)

1918, Arranmore, (Donegal)

1919, Wicklow Head, (Wicklow)

1923, Broadhaven, (Mayo)

Coinciding with the establishment of a lighthouse on Inishtearaght in the Blasket Island group, some 14 nautical miles (25km) to the north-west, the upper Skellig light was discontinued in 1870, and the lower light was altered to have a flashing character – which is still the means

Left: Joanie Cahill-O'Sullivan at Portmagee. She was a teacher to the lighthouse children on Skellig, c. 1889.
(photo courtesy
W. Harrington)

Right: James Martin King – the last child to be born on Skellig on 30 October 1897.
(Photo courtesy V. King)

of distinguishing one lighthouse from another. In 1909 the latest type of paraffin vapour incandescent burner was installed, as well as a new lens of dioptric type – that is to say, a lens made of a set of prisms placed around the light to focus it into a horizontal beam.

Such a lens also held the secret of the flashing effect. The whole optical assembly, revolving around a steady light source at a fixed speed, gave the impression of a flash as the beam passed through the observer's point of view.

Apart from the value of having such navigation aids on such outposts, the presence of knowledgable lighthouse men on site was a lifesaving bonus: On Michaelmas Day 1902, a Portmagee seine-boat which had been fishing by the Skellig was wrecked at the island's landing while the crew were ashore for a rest. The sudden wind which had done the damage also prevented help from coming for a week. Meanwhile, the Skellig larder had extra mouths to feed and the marooned fishermen had ample time to reflect on the tradition that nobody goes fishing on Michaelmas Day …

Further assistance to mariners was provided by Skellig lighthouse men in November 1916, and for their part in helping rescue two boatloads of survivors from the S.S. Marina, the three keepers were awarded £1 (€1.27) each from the Board of Trade and one guinea (€1.05) each from the Marina's owners.

The Second World War brought its share of conflict to the Skellig area. Dogged aircraft encounters and bombings of allied merchant vessels were frequent occurrences, but neutrality concerns maintained a blanket of silence on most such events.

One of the few incidents to be recorded was an aerial dogfight within sight of the Skelligs on 5 March 1941 – which resulted in the loss of an

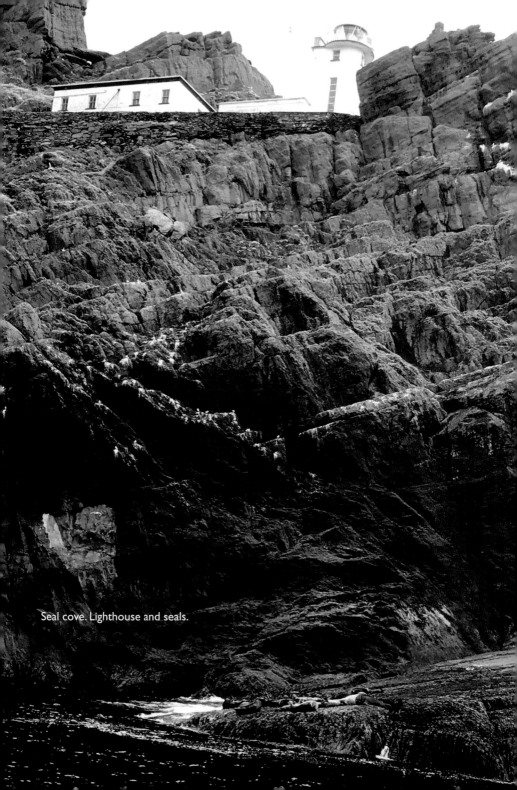

Seal cove. Lighthouse and seals.

The Vega 4-tier LED light.

unidentified aircraft. It crashed into the sea some three nautical miles (5.5km) south of Skellig. A subsequent search by an Irish Lights tender and the Fenit lifeboat yielded only an empty rubber life-raft, but fifty-three years later, 20th July 1994, a local fishing boat, the *Rose Crest*, hauled up the aircraft's propeller in its trawl. This artefact rests today in Valentia's Skellig Experience visitor centre where its story is featured. The only other Skellig-area war incident to be thoroughly researched and published was the loss of an American Liberator bomber, VB-110-PB4Y-1, which hit Skellig Michael and crashed into the sea near the island's north face on 27 February 1944. (See Bibliography, *The Fatal Echo*.)

Explosive fog signals – four-ounce charges detonated electrically – were introduced at the Skellig in 1914. In 1936 Mason reported a gigantic explosion which occurred when an electrical fault detonated simultaneously some 300 of these explosive charges. 'It nearly lifted the island out of the sea,' but no great harm ensued and this type of fog signal remained in use until 1953.

There was no fog at midnight on 18 November 1955 when the ninety-tonne French trawler, St. Yvel, ran headlong into the Skellig. She was heading home with a full cargo of fish when she hit the northern side of the rocks, where the lighthouse is not visible. Luckily there was no loss of life. Although the St. Yvel began to sink immediately, Valentia lifeboat managed to tow her from the 80m depths of the Skellig to the comparative safety of Valentia harbour before she finally went down.

Had it happened a few years earlier, the outcome might have been different because December 1951 saw some of the worst weather that the Skellig has ever recorded. On 27 December, a wave broke the glass of the

Fulmar's eye view.

lighthouse lantern – 53m above the sea – flooding the light and causing extensive damage. It was 3rd January 1952 before a relief crew of fitters with new lighting equipment could be landed on the rock.

Bill Dumigan, long-retired from the lighthouse service, recalled that Skellig accident: 'I was winding the light-machine when the lantern was smashed and I received a cut forehead from the broken glass ... During the storm we also lost our boat-landing and cargo derrick; all the stanchions leading to the landing were bent and the road was ripped away.'

But worse tragedy was to hit Skellig lighthouse. On 22 August 1956, keeper Seamus Rohu was reported missing from Skellig. His colleagues and other helpers searched the island over and over again. Valentia lifeboat and the lighthouse service vessel, *Valonia*, searched the sea around the rock for days, but all in vain.

By and large, the 1826 structure of the lower lighthouse remained unchanged for some 140 years. In 1964 the first step in a modernisation programme was taken with the installation of a powerful diesel derrick at Cross Cove, 42m above the sea, to be used for landing hundreds of tonnes of building materials; 1965 saw the beginning of the reconstruction: The two old dwellings were made into one and – as of old – the now-enlarged flat roof would be the sole source of water, a manual valve directing clean rainwater for consumption into one holding tank and any salt-contaminated water – adequate for other purposes – into another. A new bathroom with hot and cold water was provided, and oil-fired central heating installed throughout. The old interior plaster walls were studded and lined with a decorative Formica panel finish. A bedroom was provided for each keeper and two spare bedrooms for visiting tradesmen. An office was included for the principal keeper. Two Lister diesel engines would provide electric power throughout the building.

On 24 May 1966 a small temporary lantern with an electric flashing light was mounted on a nearby spur of rock, and the main light, which had guided mariners for 140 years, was extinguished. The old tower was swiftly demolished and shovelled into the sea, together with – regrettably – many old logbooks and allied papers which would have been useful to researchers today. On the site a new reinforced-concrete tower took shape – with an engine room and battery room, a workshop and an oil pump-room with a seven-year fuel supply. The lens system of 1909, which was still in perfect condition, was re-installed and now, for the first time, the lantern boasted a three-kilowatt electric lamp.

This new light, with its characteristic triple flash every ten seconds, an

The great Skellig lens system, powering the lighthouse beam since 1909, is idle now, having yielded to today's LED lighting technology.

intensity of 1,800,000 candelas and its visible range of 26 nautical miles (48km), came into operation on 25 May 1967. The total cost was £49,000 (€62,217)

But that powerful light would, in turn, be replaced. In pursuit of efficiency, the 3KW lamp would be reduced a 1kW version and the character of the light reduced from one (triple) flash every 10 seconds to a 15-second period. Its visible range was proportionally reduced to 19 nautical miles (35 km).

The Skellig lighthouse service of recent generations was a far cry from the original, not alone in construction, comfort and equipment but also, for instance, in matters of staff transport. One remembers the industrious lighthouse relief vessels – the *Deirdre*, the *Nabro*, the *Alexandra*, the *Valonia* and, later, the more sophisticated ships, the Granuaile, Ierne, Isolda and Atlanta – steaming around the coast on their lighthouse relief rounds. One remembers the same ships weather-bound in harbour for days, perhaps weeks, while the Skellig men waited for relief and supplies. One remembers when emergencies arose at these moments to complicate the situation, and the many mercy dashes which Valentia lifeboat made to the Skellig lighthouse to bring injured men to safety. The lifeboat station files tell the exciting events – but briefly:

March 24th 1950: Lifeboat relieved Skelligs Rock.

November 15th 1953: Assistant Keeper Gillan injured at Skellig. Landed by Valentia lifeboat.

April 4th 1954, Captain Martin, Engineer of Irish Lights, ill on Skellig for seven days, was taken ashore by Valentia lifeboat after relief tender, *Valonia*, had failed to land in four attempts.

June 15th 1963: Skellig keeper very ill. Taken off by Valentia lifeboat.

October 25th 1965: Injured carpenter taken off Skellig by Valentia lifeboat.

Two later service reports of that era offer more detail:

October 7th 1972: At 11.00 GMT Captain Greenly of Irish Lights telephoned Valentia lifeboat Hon. Sec., requesting that 938 (Valentia lifeboat, Rowland Watts) be launched to take an injured light-keeper off the Skellig rock. Also requested that a temporary keeper be landed in his place. Lifeboat slipped her mornings at 12.15 GMT with boarding boat in tow. Reached Skellig Rock at 14.10 GMT. Using boarding boat, the temporary keeper was landed on Skellig pier and the injured man was brought on board. 938 arrived back to Valentia at 16.20 GMT where Dr. Twomey was waiting to give medical assistance.

February 7th 1974. At 09.00 GMT, Captain Harrison Irish Lights, Dublin, telephoned Valentia lifeboat Hon. Sec., seeking assistance of 938 to take light-keeper, Brian Regan, off the Skellig Rock as his father had died. Captain Harrison explained that there was no helicopter available for the relief. At 10.00 GMT, 938 slipped her mornings and with the large boarding boat in tow, sailed for Skellig Rock. Lifeboat 2nd Coxn, Des Lavelle, volunteered to act as relief light-keeper for a week and was landed on Skellig Rock via the man-derrick as a heavy swell ruled out a pier landing. 14.30 GMT, Keeper Brian Regan was similarly taken on board by man-derrick. 17.30 GMT, 938 back at Valentia pier.

A change of lighthouse policy in 1969 saw the Skellig 'shore dwellings' on Valentia closed and sold, the lighthouse families free to move away to live where they pleased, and the introduction of a fortnightly helicopter service from Castletownbere would fly the lighthouse-keepers to and from the Skellig helipad in a matter of minutes.

Lighthouse communications made noticeable strides in that era also: In 1970, the men on Skellig had, for the first time, the luxury of a telephone, 02720097 – linked by VHF beam with the mainland exchange in Castletownbere. Before this they had only the shipping-band radio-telephone for communication with other lighthouse establishments, or with shipping, or, in an emergency, with Valentia (Coastguard) Radio Station.

But before that, before the advent of radio to Skellig? They had semaphore signals! With a large white-washed patch on the rock-face of the lighthouse road as a background, a Skellig semaphore signaller, with two flags or two black bats, could – on a clear day – be read by telescope from the Bull Rock lighthouse, some 13 nautical miles (22km) away, which, in turn, would relay the message ashore by similar means!

Two incidents highlight the difficulties of these early communications. In 1936, John Dore of Valentia, one of the three-man Skellig crew, fell ill, but thick fog prohibited the normal semaphore communication with Bull Rock. Distress rockets were fired that night, but to no avail. The fog persisted and the patient's condition grew worse.

The fog signal, some 500 metres away up a steep slope had to be manned by day and night. The light and the fog signal had to be maintained by night. Distress rockets had to be fired regularly and a watch had to be kept for the possibility of help from a passing vessel or the chance of a clearance and a contact with the Bull Rock.

A second night passed and the rockets were exhausted – without result. The patient was very ill, with only a basic first-aid box to succour him, and his two companions were still without sleep or even rest. What to do?

Every scrap of firewood – box, packing case or basket, every old newspaper, sack and rag was carted manually, load by load, up the steep climb to the monastery pinnacle. Oil by the bucket was added and a great bonfire was prepared. It was a whole day's work and as soon as darkness had fallen on the Skellig, assistant keeper, Jim Lavelle, set a match to his bonfire, sending flames roaring high into the air above the old monastery cells. The signal went afar. A Portmagee fisherman, Patrick 'Bonnet' O'Shea, who saw the glow in the foggy sky, understood the message and brought help in time.

Thirty-six years previously, during the fishing season of 1900, a similar fire had brought help in a similar situation. This time the Cahills' fishing boat – a six-oar 'follower' – set out from Valentia to answer the Skellig distress, and although most details of the successful rescue are forgotten, the sequel to it is still told in Portmagee and Valentia: when the rescue boat landed in Portmagee after its 24-mile (44km) mercy mission, the police sergeant stood in the doorway of the public house and refused to give the oarsmen admission because it was 'off hours'. Undaunted, they boarded their boat again and rowed the further 8km to Knightstown, where 'Galvin' gave them the freedom of the house!

Freedom of another house, the Skellig lighthouse – where generations of visiting boatmen always received a welcome, where the kettle was always boiling – be it on the modern cooker of later times or the coal fire of earlier days, where strong tea was always liberally dispensed, where friendship and chat of kindred souls always flowed richly – passed into history on 22nd April 1987: Skellig lighthouse watch-keepers of the final hours of 161 years and 129 days, Paddy Dirrane, Aidan Walsh and Michael O'Regan saw the station switched to fully automatic operation, unattended, unmanned, padlocked...

Not only was the lighthouse locked up, but the entire island! Preparation for this closure had included the erection of two massive masonry pillars on the roadway near the landing place with two great, insurmountable steel gates, embellished with barbed wire fortifications. It conveyed both a symbolic and concrete finality to the long-trodden route of pilgrim, boatman and appreciative Skellig visitor... The planned transfer of the island – excluding the lighthouse tower and its related dwellings – to the Office of Public Works would follow.

But nature didn't see the closure as being quite as final as that: In November of the same year, a great storm swept every vestige of gates and pillars into the ocean without a trace! Without trace, at least, until the following spring, when a team of divers located the battered remains and finally gave them an appropriate home in the Skellig Experience Centre on Valentia!

What changes the Skellig light has seen – advancing from the six-year construction feat of the 1820s, to the Argand oil lamps and parabolic reflectors of 1826 to the paraffin vapour incandescent lamps and magnificent, dioptric, rotating lens of 1909, to the totally rebuilt lower lighthouse with its 3kw lamp and twin Lister diesel engines of 1966, to the huge eco-power unit of fifty battery-charging solar panels of October 2001, to the 'lighthouse' of today:

Within the tower, the great rotating triple lens assembly of 1909 is now stationary. Once a virtual kaleidoscope of refracted light spectra, but now wrapped mummy-like in layers of white fabric to keep sunlight – and any consequent heat magnification – at bay, it is but a hidden artefact of another era. The diesel engines are silent, the 50 solar panels on the roadside are idle. Mounted on a small pedestal on the tower balcony is the ultimate Skellig light – a 4-tier Vega LED lantern, battery-powered and charged by six small solar panels on the balcony railings. In appearance, this lamp is no more than a hat-sized unit, but with its character of three white flashes every fifteen seconds and its range of twelve nautical miles, it continues to serve the mariners of today as did its predecessors since 4th December 1826.

The North Station roadside wall repairs of 2018, including newly-quarried capping stones from Valentia.

Bridled guillemot.

CHAPTER SIX

SEABIRDS

The Skellig rocks, Skellig Michael and Small Skellig, situated far from city, industry and commercial shipping lanes, may be Europe's ideal seabird sanctuary, yet the inhabitants – though well able to deal with vagaries of nature – still have to contend with the depredations of man that come in the form of plastic detritus. It can float; it can blow with the wind; it can accumulate a thousand miles away from where-ever it was discarded. And it can kill oceanic wildlife.

It is no comfort to us to read that 90% of the plastic in the oceans of the world emanates from just ten rivers – eight in Asia and two in Africa. Nor is this statistic any cause for complacency in Ireland; a local beach clean-up on a Sunday afternoon would be a minimum personal penance that may – to some small extent – absolve one's part in the collective sin of pollution and help all to enjoy the birds of Skellig while they continue to enjoy their surroundings.

For much enjoyment there is: The relative clumsiness of many of Skellig's seabirds, and the fact that some cannot readily take-off from level

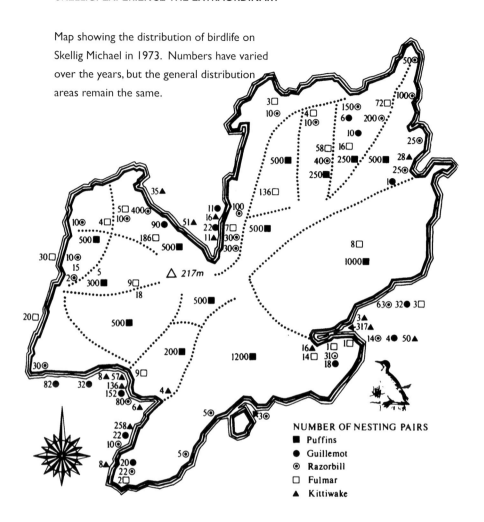

Map showing the distribution of birdlife on Skellig Michael in 1973. Numbers have varied over the years, but the general distribution areas remain the same.

NUMBER OF NESTING PAIRS
■ Puffins
● Guillemot
◉ Razorbill
□ Fulmar
▲ Kittiwake

ground but must launch themselves from a ledge to become airborne, led to an early legend that some mysterious magnetism held the birds on the island!

We can dismiss such theories today! In any event, the Skellig birds' terrestrial drawbacks are more than balanced by their great skill in the air and on, or beneath, the waves.

GANNET – SULA BASSANA

Irish: *Gainéad*; **French:** *Fou de bassan*; **German:** *Basstölpel*;
Swedish: *Havssula*; **Dutch:** *Jan van Gent.*

Pride of place in the birdlife of the area must go to the gannet, which inhabits the Small Skellig rock to the relative exclusion of all other species. If there are some of the smaller seabirds on the lower ledges it is only because these particular perches do not offer enough space for the heavy, goose-sized gannets. Every other site on this precipitous 6.5-hectare, 135m crag is taken up by the island's gannets – the latest count (2014) recording 35,294 AOS (Apparently Occupied Sites) – which makes Small Skellig the second largest of the world's twenty-three gannet colonies.

First mention of the Small Skellig gannetry was in 1700. In 1748 the gannet population was 'an incredible number', and from then onwards the estimated figures fluctuated considerably.

Gannets on Small Skellig (with Skellig Michael in the background).

1828 – 500 pairs

1880 – 30 pairs

1882 – 150 pairs

1906 – 15,000 pairs

1913 – 8,000 pairs

1941 – 10,000 pairs

1969 – 20,000 pairs

1995 – 27,214 AOS (Apparently Occupied Sites)

2004 – 29,683 AOS

2014 – 35,294 AOS

Today, there are 'No Vacancies' on Small Skellig; every available ledge is fully booked!

The gannet is obviously in a very strong position now, and one can only suggest that the fluctuations in the colony's early history were due to 'harvesting'. About 150 years ago, gannets were fetching between 1s.8d. and 2s.6d. (9c–16c) each, and as late as 1869 the Small Skellig was rented annually for the taking of feathers and young gannets - a source of warm bedding and substantial meals!

In that era, at breeding time, the rock was guarded by a boat-crew of twelve men, 'well paid by the man who owned it', but this deterrent was inadequate, and Dunleavy – in Thomas O'Crohan's *The Islandman* – tells an exciting tale of one unauthorised gannet raid that ended in bloodshed.

'This time a boat set out from Dunquin at night with eight men in her, my father among them, and they never rested till they got to the rock at daybreak. They sprang up it and fell to gathering the birds into the boat at full speed. And it was easy to collect a load of them for every single one of these young birds was as heavy as a fat goose. As they were turning the point of the rock to strike out into the bay, what should they see coming to meet them but the guard boat. They hadn't seen one another till that moment'.

Then the activity began. The guards tried to take the Dunquin boatmen prisoners, but '… some of them sprang on board and they fell to hitting at one another with oars and hatchets, and any weapon they could find in the boat till they bled one another like a slaughtered ox.'

Although outnumbered by twelve to eight, the Dunquin men won the fight and eventually got back to their own harbour with their boatload of gannets intact. When the vanquished guard boat reached its base, two men were dead, and the other ten were sent into hospital. 'After that they were less keen on that sort of chase and the guard was taken off the rock'.

Gannet harvesting, it would appear, still goes on in the Hebrides of Scotland in this age; the people of Ness on the northern tip of Lewis outraged conservationists worldwide by announcing The World Guga

Skellig's famous gannetry, with thousands of gannets vying for space on the precarious ledges.

(gannet chick) Eating Championship! One might think this to be a tasteless April Fool joke, but the date of the feature in *The Guardian* is 27th January 2014.

Even though the gannets do not lay until April or later, the nesting site is claimed immediately on return from migration in February and is guarded by one or other of the partners for the next six months. And this is hardly without reason. In any colony where thieving, predatory scavengers like herring gulls or black-blacked gulls are in attendance, any unattended property – preferably edible – is unlikely to survive very long.

Other hazards a-plenty threaten the gannet world – not least their choice of nest-building material.

The gannet makes a large, high nest of weeds and all sorts of floating rubbish – nowadays largely plastic materials. Plastic picnic cutlery is found in gannets' nests, likewise components of ballpoint pens! A Skellig gannet has been seen flying homewards past Skellig Michael, carrying a farm-sized (empty!) plastic bag! Such an item – that may weigh 75 grams and measure some 60x40cm – is adequate testimony to the gannet's wing power and aerobatic skill in getting airborne with such a cargo! More commonly, the gannet's pursuit of nest-building materials such as buoyant scraps of plastic fishing net, ropes and twine, will lead to fights about the goods, often resulting in entanglement and death unless some kindly boatman may happen to pass the way, may happen notice the fuss that other gannets create, circling overhead when one of their kin is in difficulty on the sea, and may be able to catch the victim or victims and set them free? But beware: The gannet will not thank you for this succour; its razor sharp bill will draw blood without compunction!

Gannets lay only one egg per season – dull, greenish-white in colour.

When hatched, the chick is snow-white, but its true feathers are first black and later mottled, and only in its fourth year is the full adult plumage is attained – pure white with bold black wingtips and yellow head. The mature gannet is 0.9m in length, with a long neck, long pointed bill, pointed tail and long narrow wings. The wingspan is almost 1.9m.

First-year gannets migrate in November to west-African waters or even into the Mediterranean, but in successive years they travel much shorter distances, the older birds reaching only as far as the Bay of Biscay, thus ensuring an early return to reclaim a favourite nesting site, while the juveniles, which shall not be adults or breeders for four years, wander farther afield, and may not be seen in Skellig waters till mid summer. Occasional record-breaking travellers are noted; a young gannet ringed on Small Skellig in 1968 was subsequently recovered on the coast of Brazil!

Gannet needing help.

The gannet's flight is usually direct and low with frequent gliding, the wingtip following – within millimetres – the contour of every ripple on every wave of every swell, but while feeding it wheels high in the air and will plunge into the sea upon its prey from 30m or more. Evolution has designed the gannet well for this violent activity. It has no external nostrils, no real tongue, and has an intricate pneumatic system of air-cushion shock absorbers throughout its body.

The 'Changing of the Guard' at the nest when the gannet returns from a fishing trip is a highly ceremonious show – which is not confined just to breeding time. Both birds stand face to face, wings half open, bowing to each other and knocking their bills together with much contented grunting. No doubt it could be a very graceful affair if they had enough space, but in the crowded conditions of Small Skellig, any protruding wingtip or tail which encroaches by a feather on a neighbour's territory is liable to provoke a sharp stab of retaliation – upsetting the whole ceremony.

For two months the gannet chick remains in the nest, pampered and grossly over-fed. Then it is deserted and starves for two weeks before it plucks up the courage to quit the nest. If the young bird survives this first venture, which generally involves a headlong tumble down rocks, ledges and gulleys, it has a fair chance of living to an age of forty years.

During its life the gannet will touch no other land but its breeding station. A gannet seen anywhere else – on beach, rock or shore is injured or dying. One dead gannet collected recently as part of a study had died through choking on a length of plastic pipe – an item of seaborne trash which it may have mistaken for a mackerel, herring or garfish. Only one report of a gannet ever fishing inland refers to an Antrim lake sighting on a stormy day in 1932.

The Small Skellig, virtually inaccessible, and generally regarded as out-of-bounds, has been leased long-term by the Irish Wildbird Conservancy as an official seabird sanctuary. Only occasional studies take place there: On one July day in 1972, 671 young gannets were ringed and released, and – in line with modern data collection methods – a Small Skellig project of 11th July 2011 fitted each of six gannets with a GPS tag attached to one feather. A later passing cruise, armed with a directional radio scanner– would retrieve the gannets' travel data. The feather and the GPS device would ultimately fall off harmlessly.

PUFFIN – FRATERCULA ARCTICA

Irish: *Puifín*; **French:** *Macareux moine*; **German:** *Papageitaucher*; **Swedish:** *Lunnefågel*; **Dutch:** *Papegaaiduiker*.

The puffin is one of the auk family – black and white saltwater divers

Cleared for takeoff!

with short, wide wings. Their flight is fast and whirring, seldom for long in a straight line. Puffins also use their wings to swim underwater, and they have been noted by divers as deep as 15m.

On Skellig Michael, puffins occupy every level, digging nesting holes, occupying crevices under boulders or usurping convenient rabbit burrows from which the rightful owners may be forcibly ejected. Only one egg is laid, round in shape and whitish in colour with light grey/brown spots. When the puffin chick is six weeks old it is deserted by the parents to fend for itself and to make its own way to sea. Many of them don't get there; black-backed and herring gulls are ever on the prowl for an unwary puffin – chick or adult.

Man has been a predator too: Up to the beginning of the 20th century, puffins were captured in great numbers. Their plumage was a valuable article of trade and the young birds, well salted, were regarded as a delicacy. Two salted puffins could fetch a 'peck' of meal on the market.

The fisherman returns.

Peeping puffin.

The adult puffin is easily recognised on land or at sea: black plumage above, white below, grey cheeks and bright orange feet. But its bill is the most conspicuous summer feature – bright red, blue and yellow, laterally flattened and very strong. In appearance the puffin, which is 30cm in length, is stumpy and big-headed with an awkward, upright, shuffling gait. Assembled at evening time on every convenient tussock or rock platform, puffins are likened to portly gentlemen sitting in conference or sub committee! Gentlemanly they may appear, but in a tussle over a nesting site or nesting material they can fight fiercely. Such an engagement has been noted on Skellig – where two puffins, locked in combat – with razor-sharp bills and needle-like claws – tumbled and bounced on every step and stone from Christ's Saddle down to the lighthouse road without pause or let-up in the conflict!

At the end of March, when the flocks of puffins arrive back at Skellig from their North Atlantic wanderings, they first swim around the rock for some days, not approaching very near. Then, in the evening dusk, a few – only a few – will venture ashore to spend the night. Finally, in mid-April, in the course of a couple of days, the whole flock will settle on the island and take up residence. Skellig will now be over-run with puffins until the first week in August when, in response to some great unanimous decision, the puffins will depart as suddenly as they arrived –to spend all winter, day and night, on the wide Atlantic Ocean.

But there is method to their winter wanderings: Studies conducted by the Coastal and Marine Research Centre at University College Cork have tracked the Skellig puffins' movements by attaching a tiny geolocator tracking device, weighing only 1.5 grams, to some departing Skellig birds at season's end. Of 27 birds tagged in the study, 10 returnees provided details of the recorded travels: A transatlantic track to Canadian waters – where several months' food supply of oil-rich capelin is available! Thereafter, they return to the North East Atlantic, west of Biscay, until March signals time to go home to Skellig.

RAZORBILL – ALCA TORDA

Irish: *Crosán*; **French:** *Petit pingouin*; **German:** *Tordalk*; **Swedish:** *Tordmule*; **Dutch:** *Alk*.

The razorbill, also of the auk family, is 40cm in length, with black above and white underparts. The bill is almost black in colour, laterally compressed and has a conspicuous white line across the centre. In appearance, the razorbill has a heavy head and a short thick neck. It looks rather squat while swimming and generally carries its tail cocked up.

From March to August the razorbills are on the Skellig, although some early-comers return at the end of January. The ledges below the road at Cross Cove and near the lighthouse at Seal Cove are well-popu-

Razorbill.

lated nesting sites.

One egg – a buff/blue colour, spotted with brown – is laid on the bare rock ledge without the benefit of any semblance of a nest, but, unlike the puffin, the razorbill tends its young for a long period - even after the chick has abandoned the nesting site and headed to sea.

GUILLEMOT – URIA AALGA

Irish: *Forach*; French: *Guillemot de troil*; German: *Trottellumme*; Swedish: *Sillgrissla*; Dutch: *Zeekoet*.

The guillemot is an inoffensive bird with little aggressive appearance, living by its underwater fishing, and its eggs and young are a constant target for gulls and other predators. Black or very dark brown above, white below, it is 42cm in length. A slender, more pointed bill and a thinner neck distinguish it from the razorbill.

The guillemot makes no nest, but lays its single egg in mid-May on the

Guillemot group.

inaccessible, crowded ledges at Blindman's Cove, Cross Cove and Seal Cove. The egg varies very much in colour from brown to green or white, blotched and streaked with brown, but its distinct pear shape cannot be mistaken. This shape generally prevents the egg from rolling off its unprotected ledge, but accidents do occur...

An uncommon variation of this species – the bridled guillemot – with its distinctive white eye-stripe, has often been noted on the crowded ledges of Cross Cove.

KITTIWAKE – RISSA TRIDACTYLA

Irish: *Staidhséar*; **French:** *Mouette tridactyle*; **German:** *Dreizehenmöwe*; **Swedish:** *Tretåig mås*; **Dutch:** *Drieteenmeeuw*.

On Skellig Michael the kittiwake is the noisiest bird. It nests on the ledges above the landing and at Cross Cove and Seal Cove, and seems to spend its summer screaming madly at the world at large. The voice is loud and clear and cannot be mistaken: 'kitt-i-wake … kitt-i-wake'…

The kittiwake is very much an open-sea species, which only once – in the year 1938 – has been seen inland. The wings and mantle are ash grey and the remainder of the plumage is pure white. It is distinguished from the common gull, which is a similar size, 40cm in length, by solid black triangular wingtips, olive/brown legs, an unmarked, yellow bill and a dark eye.

The kittiwake, having spent the winter on the open sea, returns to the Skellig in March – although the lighthouse records for 1972 show that some kittiwakes returned as early as 26 December – and its three eggs, stone-coloured, spotted with grey and brown, are laid at the end of May. The kittiwake makes a sturdy nest of weeds and roots, and these building materials are commonly the subject of prolonged, noisy battles over the

Kittiwake at home.

Cramped quarters for kittiwakes.

ownership of the most insignificant scraps – notwithstanding the ready availability of such goods on every side!

Kittiwake numbers are declining generally. Skellig counts have dropped from 1,031 pairs in the 1990s to 573 pairs in 2014. But this is hardly as disastrous as the losses reported in St Kilda and the Western Isles of Scotland where, since season 2000, populations have fallen by 96%.

Why this disaster? The proffered answer to this question is the disappearance of their sand eel food source. But that answer only leads to another question ... and another...

At best, chick mortality must be very high in typical kittiwake communities like Skellig's Cross Cove. Here, on the narrow ledges, even the normal daily activity can frequently result in eggs or chicks being knocked over the edge and into the sea. It was here too, in 2014, that the down-draught from a helicopter on a reconnaissance flight for Star

Wars, dislodged kittiwake chicks from their nests and hurried them to their deaths in the waters below.

Strangely, the fortnightly helicopter flights for the lighthouse service personnel between 1969 and 1987 never created similar disasters...

STORM PETREL – HYDROBATES PELAGICUS

Irish: *Mairtíneach*; **French:** *Pétrel tempête*; **German:** *Sturmschwalbe*; **Swedish:** *Stromsvala*; **Dutch:** *Stormvogeltje.*

At 15cm in length, the storm petrel is the smallest European seabird, visiting land only while breeding. It is sooty black, with a conspicuous white rump and a square black tail.

Storm petrels occupy every tiny nook and cranny on Skellig Michael but they are seldom seen by day as they remain hidden in their nests, or far out to sea. At dusk they appear, flitting just above the waves, feet dangling so low that they seem to be running on the water. Surface feeders all, petrels too are high on the list of plastic victims.

The storm petrel amidst the greenery near its burrow (Photo: Michael O'Clery (Illaunammil).)

The wall repairs and pointing closed
the petrels' nest-site options.

Following their winter migrations in the waters of South Africa, storm petrels return to the Skellig at the end of April, and by the end of June one oval egg – white, with rust spots – is laid in a burrow or deep within the crevices of any stonework. Incubation takes five or six weeks and during this time the bird will often wander great distances for food, leaving the egg or the chick un-attended for days. Many storm petrels – many thousands, perhaps – found generations of homes within the stonework of Skellig's roadside wall – only to lose them in recent years through extensive, mortared renovations to the masonry. If a recently-created low wall near Skellig's North Station – containing some intentional chinks – is an offer of alternative accommodation to the petrels it is pitifully inadequate.

Occasionally the call of the storm petrel – a purring sound with a 'hiccough' at the end – will lead you to its nest site – but hardly to sight of the bird; sooty black at the end of a dark burrow equals invisibility!

The storm petrel, also known as Mother Carey's Chicken, takes to the open sea again in October. They are never seen inland – except after some fierce storms in 1839 and 1891 when these birds were strewn dead over miles of countryside.

A distant relation of the tiny storm petrel – very distant in size and in habitat – caused a stir in Birdwatching circles when it appeared in Skellig waters in May 2018. This was a black browed albatross.

Normally a resident of the southern oceans, where some 160,000 pairs breed on the Falkland Islands, the albatross is rarely seen in the NE Atlantic. One albatross sighting was reported by the survey ship, *Celtic Explorer*, 160 nautical miles SW of Mizen Head on February 29th 2012. Another albatross took up residence with the gannet colony in the Hebrides of Scotland in 1974 and 1975!

But the Irish coast's fine weather and calm seas of May/June 2018 would have been but an impediment to the albatross. This is a bird best suited to storm, wave and swell.

MANX SHEARWATER – PUFFINUS PUFFINUS

Irish: *Cánóg*; **French:** *Puffin des anglais*; **German:** *Schwarzschnabel – Sturmtaucher*; **Swedish:** *Mindre lira*; **Dutch:** *Noordse Pijlstormvogel.*

The Manx shearwater is very clumsy on land and is seldom seen there by day. Even on fine, calm nights they prefer to hide away, and only on cloudy, windy nights when the shearwaters venture out in their full force and full voice can a guess of the local population can be formed.

They are sometimes seen in groups or rafts, particularly towards evening time when large flocks gather on the water near the breeding ground. Sooty black above, white underneath and 35cm in length, the

Manx shearwater. Rarely seen on land by day.

shearwater is recognised easily by its distinctive flight – very low over the sea, following the contours of each wave, gliding frequently on stiff wings with only occasional wing beats.

In March the shearwaters return from their winter migration in South American waters. They breed in burrows and will use the same burrow year after year. One white, oval egg – very large in relation to the bird – is laid at the end of April and both birds sit, but frequently the nest is left unattended for days while the birds forage far afield for food.

In the summer of 1972 one shearwater had its nest at the foot of the altar steps in the Large Oratory of the Skellig monastery, quite indifferent to visitors and cameras! Parenthood is a long task for the shearwaters: Incubation takes seven-and-a-half weeks, and the chick remains in the nest for a further ten-and-a-half weeks, by which time it has become far heavier and fatter than the parent birds. Eventually it is deserted and endures a week's starvation before it decides to venture forth to the sea. And this big initial adventure must be made under the cover of darkness; the young shearwater is so helpless on land that it would be devoured by gulls if it showed itself by day.

FULMAR – FULMARUS GLACIALIS

Irish: *Fulmaire;* **French:** *Petrel glacial;* **German:** *Eissturmvogel;*
Swedish: *Stormfågel;* **Dutch:** *Noordse Stormvogel.*

Prior 1900, the fulmar was a rare visitor to Ireland from Northern regions. But its numbers and breeding stations were rapidly spreading southwards, and in 1913, RM Barrington reported twelve pairs nesting for the first time on Skellig Michael. Some seventy birds arrived in 1914, and about 100 in 1915. Thus the colony was established and from Skellig they spread out to other local rocks and cliffs.

The fulmar finally found peace in this period and this area. Only thirty years previously some 12,000 fulmars were 'harvested' annually on St Kilda alone – 115 birds per every member of the population. One report put it this way: 'No bird is of such use. The fulmar supplies oil for their lamps, down for their beds, a delicacy for their tables, a balm for their wounds and a medicine for their distempers …'

The fulmar is gull-like in appearance, 50cm in length, with a white head and a grey back, wings and tail. But here the similarity ends. The fulmar has a thick neck, a short, hooked, yellow bill with conspicuous tubed nostrils, and a distinctive, stiff-winged flight with wonderful mastery of air currents.

Fulmar on the wing.

Being surface feeders, fulmars are particularly prone to ingestion of plastic – a fact that stems from their high dependence on a sense of smell to locate food sources. Research at the Galway-Mayo institute of Technology involving studies of dead seabirds has found that – of 250 dead birds examined – 20% had plastic in their stomachs. The Fulmar was the most effected: 93% of those examined had swallowed plastic – many to the extent that that they had starved to death.

Related studies of all tube-nosed seabirds – including fulmars – undertaken in Monterey bay and Bodega bay, California, called on unlikely partners for assistance – the Robert Mondavi Institute for Wine and Food Services! Scientists here normally focus on the fragrance and flavour of wine, but confirmed in this study that common plastics, particularly polyethylene and polypropylene, immersed for some weeks in seawater, support an algae that exudes a sulphurous scent like krill. And krill is a tasty treat on any seabird's menu...

Fulmars are at Skellig from January to September. They nest at all levels, frequently in easily accessible places on rock or greenery, both parents taking four-day duty tours incubating the single white egg, which is enveloped completely in underfeathers. Easily accessible, yes, but the fulmar will eject mouthfuls of foul-smelling oil at any curious intruder who comes too near.

Fulmars, seen for the first time in a new area, are not necessarily nesting; it is their habit to 'prospect' a cliff very thoroughly for a few seasons before deciding to breed there.

Skellig is not just for seabirds: Wrens are here and wheatears, rock pipits, choughs and ravens, and generally the monarch of all is a peregrine falcon – unless a white tailed sea eagle makes a brief visit, as happened on

26th September 2007! This uncommon wanderer, probably from newly introduced stock in Killarney National Park, stayed a few days, provided novel bird-watching opportunities for lighthouse technicians, Richard Foran and Pat Stewart, caused avid interest among Skellig visitors and created conspicuous disquiet among Small Skellig's gannets!

But disquiet is a given norm for wildlife: Dare we pray today that Skellig shall never be linked with such environmental horror-words as Torrey Canyon, Betelgeuse, Amoco Cadiz, Exxon Valdes, Sanchi... Dare we wish that some miracle may eventually diminish the life span of discarded plastic and rid land and sea of this menace? And dare we hope that all those beautiful Skellig creatures, braving autumn and winter on a wide, wild ocean shall return safely in spring and come ashore once more to reproduce their own kind?

Black browed albatross at Skellig, 30.05.18.
(photo by John N. Murphy).

Seabirds: Skellig Michael	Count unit					
	AOS (Apparently Occupied Site)	1969	1973	1990	1990/2000 /04	2014
Fulmar	AOS		588	482	761	765
Manx Shearwater	AOS (Burrow)	<10,000	<10,000		738	No count
Storm Petrel	AOS	<10,000	588		9,994	No count
Shag	AON (Nest)					2
Lesser Black-backed Gull	AOT (Territory)		28	40	15	18
Herring Gull	AOT	250	129	25	12	20
Great Black-backed Gull	AOT	12	6	6	5	6
Kittiwake	AON (Nest)		950	1,031	694	573
Guillemot	Individuals		250	266	1,422	1,625
Razorbill	Individuals		750	86	386	196
Puffin	Individuals	6,000	6,000	2,237	c.4,000	No count
Seabirds: Small Skellig						
Fulmar	AOS	10			45	
Kittiwake	AON	1120			250	
Guillemot	Individuals	579			1,129	
Razorbill	Individuals	35			68	
Gannet	AOS	20,000			29,683	35,294

Path to Blue Cove. Restored from ancient erosion, restored again following a rockfall coincidental with an offshore earthquake near County Mayo.

CHAPTER SEVEN

GEOLOGY & FLORA

These isolated Skellig crags, now surrounded by seas which are 80m deep, were once part of a great mainland landmass! The sediments of 350-million years ago became the Old Devonian Sandstone of today, making the Skelligs an integral part of the adjacent MacGillycuddy's Reeks of Kerry and the Caha mountains of west Cork. Today, the remnants of an undersea ridge still link the Washerwomen Rocks, Skellig Michael, Small Skellig, Lemon Rock and Puffin Island with the South Kerry mainland.

It was not an easy transition from a flat sediment to the creation of mountain and valley; those were violent times 100 million years later – when associated rises in sea level also created the indentations of Kenmare Bay and Bantry Bay – all the while introducing cracks and fault lines that are still conspicuous.

Several major faults occur in Skellig Michael – particularly noticeable at sea level where they penetrate the rock as conspicuous caves. While the fissures at Blind Man's Cove and Cross Cove are reasonably sheltered and accessible, the caves under the lighthouse at Seal Cove and under the

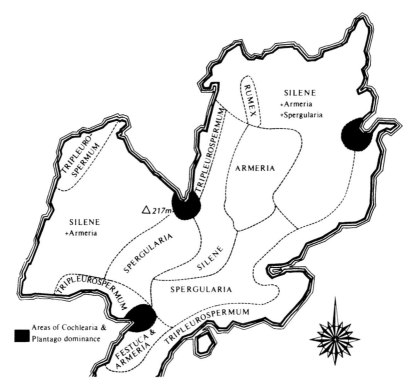

Map showing distribution of plantlife on Skellig in 1973. No major survey has been undertaken since this time.

North Landing in Blue Cove – ever influenced by the ocean swell – are deep caverns that still hold their secrets.

But clues abound: A boatman seeking an hour's rest in the total calm of a fine summer's day will often tie-up to the convenient, sea-level eye-bolts beneath the long-gone cargo derrick in Cross Cove. There, in the stillness, he shall hear a quiet gurgling of water in the cave's innermost reaches – suggesting that this fault penetrates the island at sea level and links-up with Blue Cove on the northern face or the Seal Cove caves to the west...

Likewise, at sea level on Small Skellig, daylight shines through one north/south aperture, and of the island's two other such features, the arch in the south eastern corner has become greatly enlarged in recent years as the Atlantic probes relentlessly for weaknesses. A rock fall at this spot, noted on 14th May 2011, is adequate evidence that the battle goes on.

But the ocean is not the only enemy: On June 6th 2012, a serious rock fall on the north face of Skellig Michael plunged into Blue Cove – taking part of the recently-restored northern stairway with it... This was not the work of wind or wave; the event coincided with an earthquake of Magnitude 4 in the seabed 100km west of Belmullet, Co. Mayo!

Some of the rock falls of various years, came to a rest on to the lighthouse roadway; others even damaged the cliffside wall and continued into the sea. Others of immense weight that settled on the roadway offered little remedial choice but to break the wall and heave them over the edge.

Fresh rockfall at Small Skellig, noted 14 May 2011.

The rock falls of winter 2016 and the subsequent clearance of a great assortment of related stones and loose materials in the spring of 2017 did not go to waste, however: These stones were retained and can look forward to a new life and a new duty where, in 2017, the OPW commenced refurbishment of another section of road and its clifftop wall on the route leading from the lighthouse to the old North Station.

But recycled materials do not always suffice in shape or size, and to date, some 100 heavy slate slabs – 30"x28"x3" (76x71x8cm) – to replace the lost capping stones of this roadside wall, have been delivered Skellig – some of them by helicopter!

When ever this area may open to the public is another question; the necessary work to make the area safe is monumental indeed. But it is a

Veins of quartz in Skellig's Old Devonian sandstone.

worthwhile project as the atmosphere up here amongst the choughs and the ravens in the ghostly ruins of the old lighthouse, 350 feet (106m) above the Atlantic, is precious indeed.

Geology leads to botany, and here a whole new aspect of Skellig opens up. Diarist, Crofton Croker, (1798-1854), reporting on his visit to Skellig during the lighthouse construction period in the 1820s, gave a very good description of the island – including details of his hasty departure in a looming weather change. But he made a peculiar botanical statement: 'Verdure there was none to soothe the eye of the weary pilgrim; all was nakedness and barren rock …'

Perhaps he confused Skellig Michael and Small Skellig in that report? One can still generalise and say that the vegetation of Skellig Michael is rather sparse, but this is not entirely true; there are thirty-eight species of hardy rock plants on Skellig Michael, which, in season, bloom from April onwards, providing patches of splendid greenery and colour.

All Skellig plants are rather common species – found in any sea-cliff terrain – and there is nothing which would relate directly to the earlier monastic cultivation. Although some of these common cliff plants could still supplement a basic monastic diet to some advantage, only in legend do we find reference to another botanical surprise: A miraculous crop of corn – and a miraculous supply of provisions which saved the monks from starvation until the corn could be harvested!

One wonders about this gardening exercise! Where on Skellig is there soil enough to cultivate a worthwhile crop of corn? One looks askance at the monastery garden and the limited area of Christ's saddle and wonders if the monks of old – in the climate of old, and with the determination of old – had mini gardens on every ledge!

Sea pink and sea campion on Skellig Michael.

The most conspicuous – and puzzling – development in the flora of Skellig Michael is the fact that large areas of sea pink are dying out. The whole southern face of the island, which up to 1970 was a firm stronghold of sea pink and rock sea spurrey, has become ever more denuded and has been eroded to an alarming degree. Botanists do not have an explanation for this, but far-reaching effects may well result from this change, because the tough root systems of the pinks were the main anchorage for much of the soil and otherwise loose rocks on the island's steep slopes. Sea campion has taken over much of this territory, but if rock falls are any evidence, the ongoing stability of these slopes is a major concern. Little wonder that signs advising "Beware of Falling Rocks" abound!

Small Skellig has not been extensively studied for plant life and although very little greenery is evident to the casual observer – as, no doubt, it was in Crofton Croker's time – the eight species reported in the plant lists may not be the complete picture. Indeed, the present abundance of gannets on Small Skellig may diminish the plant life even further.

PLANTS OF SKELLIG
'*' DENOTES PLANTS FOUND ALSO ON SMALL SKELLIG.

Agrostis stolonifera.	Creeping bent.	June–August
Agrostis tenuis.	Common bent.	July–August
Aira Praecox.	Early hair grass.	April–June
Anagallis arvensis.	Scarlet pimpernel.	June–August
Armeria maritima.*	Sea pink.	March–September
Asplenium marinum.	Sea spleenwort.	
Atriplex glabriuscula.	Babington's orache.	July–September
Atriplex hastata.*	Hastate orache.	August–September
Beta vulgaris.*	Sea beet.	July–September

Cerastium fontanum.	Common mouse-ear.	April–September
Cerastium tetrandrum.	Dark-green chickweed.	April–October
Cirsium vulgare	Spear thistle.	July–September
*Cochlearia officinalis.**	Common scurvy grass.	May–August
Dryoptens dilatata.	Buckler fern.	
Festuca rubra.	Red fescue.	May–June
Holcus lanatus.	Yorkshire fog.	May–August
Jasione montana.	Common sheep's bit.	May–August
Juncus bufonius.	Toad rush.	
Leontodon autumnalis.	Smooth hawkbit.	July–October
*Plantago coronopus.**	Buck's-horn plantain.	May–August
Plantago maritima.	Sea plantain.	June–August
Poa annua.	Annual meadow grass.	All year
Poa trivialis.	Rough meadow grass.	June–July
Polypodium vulgare.	Common polypody.	
Rumex acetosa.	Common sorrel.	May–June
Rumex crispus.	Curled dock.	June–October
Sagina maritima.	Sea pearlwort.	May–September
Sagina procumbens.	Common pearlwort.	May–October
Sedum anglicum.	English stonecrop.	June–August
Senecio jacobaea.	Ragwort.	June–August
*Silene maritima.**	Sea campion.	June–August
Sonchus asper.	Prickly sowthistle.	June–August
Sonchus oleraceus.	Common sowthistle.	June–August
*Spergularia rupicola.**	Rock sea spurrey.	June–September
Stellaria media.	Chickweed.	All year
Trifolium repens.	White clover.	May–October
*Tripleurospermum maritimum.**	Scentless chamomile.	July–September
Umbilicus rupestris.	Wall pennywort.	June–August

LICHEN

On Skellig, in the presence of such a feast of seascape, landscape and wildlife, one may tend to lose sight the smaller, intimate picture at one's feet – particularly lichen.

Lichens, in their various forms, mosaics and colours – from grey to green to yellow to orange to red to black – are a feature on almost every Skellig Michael rock face. The island's remote location, oceanic climate and silica-rich Old Devonian sandstone are conducive to lichen growth, and no less than 128 species were recorded (Douglass & Whelan) on Skellig Michael in summer 2009. In this context, and in relation to other small Irish and Scottish islands, Skellig is regarded as 'Nationally Important' for lichens.

Lichen is largely the product of a union – a symbiosis – between algae and fungus; the algae uses sunlight to create food and the fungus absorbs

Skellig's Old Devonian sandstone and its surrounding oceanic climate combine to offer an ideal ambience for lichen growth.

nutrients from the environment. A mini food chain exists here in the lichen world of Skellig: The copious bird droppings and the salt content of the oceanic climate nourish the lichens, snails and other invertebrates feed on the lichens, birds such as chough and raven feed on the invertebrates, and the peregrine falcon will happily feed on the chough and the raven. And the cycle begins again...

Some of Skellig's lichens are rare or scarce elsewhere.

Anaptychia ciliaris: Nationally scarce.
Amandinea coniops: Nationally scarce.
Caloplaca britannica: Nationally rare.
Caloplaca arcis: A new addition to the Irish lichen flora (2009).
Caloplaca littorea: Nationally scarce.
Lecania aipospila: Nationally scarce.

Left: Colourful Caloplaca lichen on Skellig's roadside wall.
Below: Washerwoman rocks (foreground) are the extremity of an ancient geological ridge stretching eastwards through Skellig Michael, Small Skellig, Lemon rock, Puffin Island and Kerry's Macgillacuddy reeks.

Lichen in orange and yellow almost to the ocean's edge.

Lecania aipospila: Nationally scarce.

Lecania poeltii: Rare. Previously known only in Portugal and North Africa. Found on concrete hut near the helipad.

Lecanora zosterae: Nationally scarce.

Lecidella meiococca: Nationally scarce.

Ramalina chondrina: Nationally rare; near-threatened.

Historically, throughout the world, many of the 20,000 known lichens have been used as ingredients in food, dyes, perfumes and folk medicines... Suffice, however, to say that the recipes for treating the lichen and extracting its desired products – and the wide variety of human and animal applications for which the products were recommended – would not make a good topic of conversation for a Skellig picnic lunch!

CHAPTER EIGHT

SKELLIG SEA WORLD

Cruising by Small Skellig under power or sail, and however impressed by the gannet colony, one cannot miss the island's grey seals that spend their summer days basking on the rock ledges or fishing adroitly in the surrounding seas. They are hardly resident here as these Skellig islands offer no adequate, sheltered haul-out – crucial for the breeding time in early October. Occasional seal pups have been noted in the landing cove of nearby Puffin Island, but the Blasket islands are the significant local breeding grounds.

How convenient that it is by their noses – the only part which is visible as they swim – that seals are identified: On grey seals, the conspicuously humped nose is the male telltale; the female nose is relatively straight. On Ireland's other pinniped, the common seal, a pert, upturned nose is the identification. Such a potential confusion does not exist here at Skellig; the common seal is a creature of sheltered creeks and estuaries, not of this wild ocean site.

South landing; access point for monks, early lighthouse builders – and seals.

And here is a strange 'mistake' in nature: The common seal pups, born in their sheltered havens, can swim from birth; grey seal pups, born on the wildest edges of the ocean amidst the harshness of autumnal gales cannot! As a consequence of this, estimates put mortality of grey seal pups as high as 50%.

Seals are inquisitive creatures; while you are observing the seals, you too are being observed, as big, black, be-whiskered heads pop up in the vicinity. Likewise underwater, swimming up close to a diver, the seals will stare in what appears to be stark, wide-eyed disbelief, and then dash away again – only to repeat the performance a moment later, perhaps even nibbling at the tip of a divers fin in a further gesture of curiosity

Seals are a protected species with few natural predators. Orcas come to mind, but sightings of these in local waters have been few indeed. Man, as a predator, has not always had an honourable record in the past. But at last, this more enlightened age finally offers some peace for Ireland's 7,000/9,000 grey seals and their 1,800 annual pups – and more conse-

A wary grey seal is alert to all activity.

Underwater encounters with curious seals are commonplace for those lucky enough to dive in Skellig's waters (photo courtesy Jos Audenaerd).

quent pleasure for their current human admirers.

For those of us who have the opportunity to extend our exploration of Skellig to the underwater world, there is much reward. The seals, the giant basking shark, the shoals of pollock and mackerel, the defiant lobsters, the proud crawfish and the rich colours of the anemone-clad rock faces create a silent moonscape of remarkable beauty. The whims of wind, weather and tide add to the infinite variety of this area, and it is little wonder that in the short space of years since diving has become commonplace, the name of Skellig has become famous in the diving circles of Europe – and beyond.

Skellig is a place for experienced divers only. Tidal currents can be strong around the underwater cliffs that plunge downward in jagged faces to a depth of 70m. Many factors – physical and technical – govern the time that may be spent admiring this underwater world, but cold is

Jewel anemones in fuchsia and purple provide a striking contrast to brilliant white sagartia in Skellig's vibrant underwater world (Photo courtesy Billy Rafter).

always a factor: Skellig's North Atlantic waters – at the same latitude as Canada's frozen Labrador coast – are well tempered by the Gulf Stream, but even though the surface temperature at Skellig may be 16°C on a September day, the thermoclines at a depth of 30m may be only 10°C – or lower. Nonetheless, the efficient insulation of modern diving suits can mitigate these limitations.

A quirk of Skellig weather led three Limerick divers to an interesting find in the spring of 1975:

John, Martin and Noel are with me on board the dive-boat, *Béal Bocht*. The wind is northeast, Force 3, which means that they must dive on the west side of the islands. Small Skellig, with its interesting seal coves, is the choice.

Experienced divers all, they kit up in a matter of minutes and, lamps in hand, they slip over the side and are gone.

Down the steep rock face they glide, swimming through a 3m-high forest of gold and red kelp. The yellow colours begin to disappear as they descend, then the reds... There is still ample light and horizontal visibility is 12m or more, but gradually, as daylight is filtered out by the water, everything becomes blue. The divers switch on their lamps and immediately all the glorious red and yellow sponges and the green and turquoise anemones come back to vivid life.

It is silent here. The only audible sound is the two-tone hiss of respiration and exhaust bubbles. A seal swims into view, grey and ghostly, and suddenly is gone again — totally masterful in its own environment.

At 25m, the seaweed begins to thin out and only a few barren stalks remain. A shoal of mackerel passes overhead, reducing the weak daylight to almost nil. The divers pause and watch the intricate, military-like

Brilliant jewel anemones in every colour carpet the underwater rockfaces of Skellig (Photo courtesy Paul Burton).

Even with the help of an underwater scooter, a photographer is hard-pressed to keep up with a basking shark's slowest pace.

movements of the shoal: 'Left turn. Right turn.' To some unheard command, ten thousand fish turn as one, synchronised to a fraction of a second. 'About turn. Quick March.' The shoal moves on …

Now the divers are in the bottom of a gully, 30m below the surface; there is little or no weed growing at this depth and the surrounding water is deathly still – but it is a deceptive stillness; the smooth polish on the rock face is indicative of the savage abrasions of sand and boulders during winter storms.

A spotted dogfish – lazy offshoot of the shark family – lumbers into the scene and flops down on a flat rock for a rest. Bleary-eyed and lethargic in appearance, it is reluctant to be disturbed, and even when the divers approach it moves only a few metres, and rests again.

From the dim cavern beneath a large boulder, the cold, baleful stare of a conger eel is fixed on the three approaching newcomers. Steel-blue body, white mane erect along the length of its back, the conger is powerful, fearsome and sinister-looking – but tends to mind its own business if left unmolested.

A huge angler fish, perfectly camouflaged in its grey mottling, lies on the shingle between the rocks, its mouth – almost as wide as its body-length – wide agape. A 'fishing rod' appendage dangles from its nose as a bait to entice smaller fry within range of its razor-sharp teeth. This is another one best left untouched!

A colourful green scorpion fish rests on a bed of brilliant yellow sponge, offering a splendid photo opportunity.

The divers continue along the crevasse, checking time and depth frequently. Here, is a lobster in resplendent blue; aggressive and unafraid; it raises its claws and challenges the intruders. There, in the shelter of an overhanging ledge is a fragile rose-coral in muted apricot, nearby is a crawfish in sunset red, clinging to a pointed crag. Using its powerful escape mechanism, it shoots off backwards out of sight with a few powerful thrusts of his tail. Left or right, up or down, an indescribable variety of colour blazes on every side when touched by the pencil beam of the lights.

The three companions stop, rock-still, hardly breathing. Here is an ancient anchor and some fragments of rusted chain… and a cannon… and some lead pipes… and another cannon – and another …

A wreck at the Skellig! What ship was this? When was she lost? What hardship and misery did these sailors suffer in their final hours, with only the wild Atlantic for a grave, the gaunt rocks for a headstone, and the ever-screaming gannets for a dirge?

In the boat, we have been following the progress of the divers' air bubbles, and finally the three men surface right beside our boarding ladder. 'Cannons and anchors and lead plumbing ...' They are agog with the news even before they climb out of the water. 'The cannons are about 2.5m in length ... the lead pipe is about 10cm in diameter, the anchors are long and have strange, angular flukes ...' It seemed like a big joke, and the skipper is not quite prepared to believe that after some ten years of diving and exploration in this area, the Skellig had finally yielded an unknown wreck!

Everyone joked that he wanted a cannon for his front lawn and that the lead pipe might have good value as scrap ... But that was not the way to go. The find was reported to The Receiver of Wrecks and eventually – 1996 – having received a Licence under the National Monuments (Amendment) Act, 1987, and conducting many subsequent dives on this site, nothing further of interest was located.

Nor was it easy to identify the wreck or the circumstances of her loss, but tentative pointers suggest a small vessel of the eighteenth or nineteenth century. It is possible that we are looking at the resting place of that ninety-seven-tonne, single-decked brig, owned by Shaw & Co. of Greenock, registered in Liverpool, plying between Dublin and Oporto under Captain Bernard Wade, and lost at the Skelligs on 29th October 1809 – *The Lady Nelson*.

I'm not sure that I really want to know for certain. For me, it is exciting to have one more Skellig question which does not have a concrete answer.

Seal Cove – and locals.

Skellig Experience Centre and Valentia Bridge.

CHAPTER NINE

THE SKELLIG EXPERIENCE VISITOR CENTRE

On the waterfront of Valentia Island, beside the Valentia Island bridge, stands The Skellig Experience Visitor Centre, its arched, grass-covered roof and its façade of natural local stone in perfect tune with the surrounding scenery.

Opened 1992, this concept was born out of the then concern for possible over-usage of Skellig: The Skellig Experience Centre would offer the Skellig enthusiast the option of circumnavigating the islands in a purpose-built passenger vessel and of enjoying the Skellig story through the visitor centre's indoor comfort. The centre itself became an ongoing success but the related cruise failed to prosper and was ultimately discontinued. Current cruise activity in 2017 has shown that this early cruise concept was exactly 25 years ahead its time in 1992!

The Skellig Experience Centre's exhibition 'imports' the sights, sounds and stories of the Skellig Islands across 12 miles (19km) of ocean to this readily accessible location. In line with current usage, the original building has already been extended to create additional dining space, and studies are under way regarding further up-to-date means of serving today's more discerning and more numerous visitors.

Within the exhibition, four popular Skellig themes are illustrated and discussed by means of models, graphics, artefacts and a twelve-minute audio-visual presentation in an eighty-seat theatre.

The life and times of the Early Christian monks in the island monasteries of the west coast of Ireland are included in the Visitor Centre's pre-

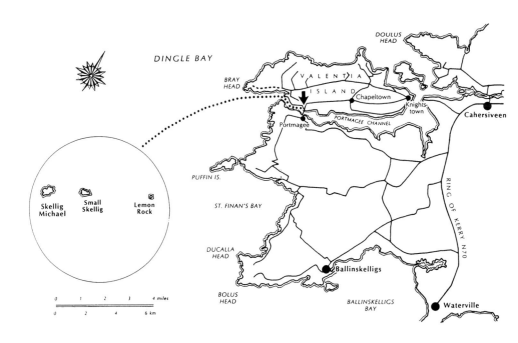

Arrow points to the location of Skellig Experience Visitor Centre.

Skellig Experience lighthouse exhibit.

sentations. A major stonework feature of this section is the hand-built, scaled-down replica of a monk's cell from Skellig Michael, including, typically, a storm petrel nesting in a chink of the stonework!

Highlighted in one related panel is the Latin text from the Annals of Ulster, recording the sacking of Skellig by the Vikings in AD823. Highlighted in another is a tiny detail of the Early Christian period: A scrap of woolen fabric – some 2.5cm square – found in an archaeological excavation of the Early Christian burial site on nearby Church Island in Valentia harbour. This cloth was not a local product - nor was it available in northern Europe! Analysis of the fabric's dye and its '2/1' weave indicated that the garment in question came from the Mediterranean or

The storm-wrecked steel gates from Skellig.

North Africa! The concept of Skellig monks wearing imported raiment merits a smile, perhaps…

In the Skellig Centre theatre, a twelve-minute video is a complete tour of Skellig on foot and from aerial and sea-borne angles, capturing the history, the facts and features of Skellig. It is a guided tour of ancient Skellig. It visits the old landing places, climbs the old stone stairways, tip-toes through the silent monastic settlement and ascends to the extreme hermit's cell at the island's South Peak. En route, the camera touches the many moods of Skellig – tranquillity, storm, isolation, peace, faith and human endeavour.

The story of Skellig lighthouses is told in a re-creation of the lighthouse duty room – how these 19th century feats of engineering were built and manned, their history, their 'lightkeepers' and their involvement in many marine incidents – from local misadventure, to shipwreck to the wartime casualties of the 1940s within sight in the surrounding seas. One such artefact is an aircraft propeller blade, relic of the now-identified Heinkel III, No. 3734, which spent fifty years underwater at a depth of some 61 meters three miles south of Skellig since the fatal wartime engagement noted by the Skellig lighthouse-men at 11.55am on 5th March 1941.

Blueprints and illustrations of the lighthouse construction work of the 1820's will impress an engineer of today: The design problems of

Skellig fleet at Portmagee marina.

road-building and rock-blasting on the sheer cliff face, the logistics of ferry, carriage and porterage of huge items of stone for wall, house and tower construction as well as related cast iron porch components for the domestic installations required imagination, skill and hard labour. Overall, this was a feat of engineering for George Halpin and a feat of workmanship for his tradesmen and labourers.

The smallest – and least noticed – exhibit in the lighthouse section recalls a very important facet of Skellig lighthouse life: It is a red-painted wooden fob, hanging on a cup-hook in the duty room. On one side it carries the script 'Tank Open' and on the other 'Tank Closed'. Bearing in mind that the station's sole water supply was rainwater from the roof, eternal vigilance was needed to ensure that only clean rainwater was collected! In normal rain, the fresh water tank was open – and the fob was turned to say so; if gales were forecast and the roof could offer only salt-contaminated water, the tank was closed, and the fob turned accordingly – always a vital reminder of the water supply status!

And this simple artefact still has relevant echoes today: Harvested rainwater may have been adequate for the needs of a three-man lighthouse crew of old, but today's resident OPW Skellig staff depend on dozens of 20-litre water drums, refilled, date-tagged, fetched and ferried from Killarney! And despite the OPW'S recent acquisition of the vacant Skellig lighthouse dwelling as staff accommodation (2018), the island's dire water situation offers no hope of comfort to the Skellig visitors' wish for a public toilet…

In the seabird section of the Skellig Experience Centre, life-size models of the coastal denizens are displayed in a realistic cliff-face habitat of native rocks and boulders. Their lives and travels are well exemplified in a panel devoted to one Skellig storm petrel:

'Stormy' received its first identification ring, No. 2365699, from David Wilson on 30th May 1966, and thereafter enjoyed some twenty-six years of long-distance ocean travel on its annual migration from Skellig's autumn waters to South Africa's sunny seas – and back…

Real eggs of real guillemots, razorbills and kittiwakes make a colourful display in this section. Not that any nests have been robbed to gather them; these eggs were salvaged by diver-and-lighthouse-man, Aidan Walsh, from the seabed at the foot of the cliff face where the birds' crowded living conditions often lead to such accidental mishaps and losses!

Colourful too are the photographic depictions of Skellig's underwater world – its rich and brilliant marine life as captured by some of Skelligs' earliest underwater visitors. Modern video clips augment the section and Skellig seals are – as always – the stars of the show.

The great steel gates that – in 1986 – sought to block access to Skellig are now part of the island's underwater story. They failed to survive the test of that year's first storm and – complete with their masonry pillars – were hurled into the sea. Thanks to the salvage work of an amateur diving expedition in 1987, today's Skellig Experience visitor can walk again through this portal of now-mangled steel and, perhaps, contemplate en route the awesome power of the Atlantic ocean that created this warped, twisted artefact.

In 2016, the Skellig Centre's souvenir shop, well stocked with a predictable range of 'normal' goods, suddenly had to find space for the appropriate souvenirs of a new era – Skellig *Star Wars* goods for Skellig *Star Wars* fans!

But, strangely, the advent of *Star Wars VII* and *VIII* to Kerry did not result in the production of any great variety of appropriate souvenirs for the subsequent thronging fans.

True, there were generic postcards and fridge magnets; true, there were T-shirts of assorted design - some even appearing in Kerry at large while 'Star Wars' was still but a local rumour in the Skellig hinterland! And yes, there were souvenir shopping bags depicting some fearsome space warrior on one side and a Disney-like logo on the other... But one had to venture to west Kerry and the environs of the Sybil head (Ceann Sibéal) shoot to find some cottage novelties like hand-made crochet porgs! Indeed, the discerning, over-laden, international traveller seeking just one novel, cover-all souvenir of his Irish odyssey to the local birthplace of *The Force Awakens* and *The Last Jedi,* might well settle for a rather mediocre, black T-shirt emblazoned with the exhortation: 'GO MBEIDH AN FÓRSA LEAT'!

The Skellig Centre's restaurant area, now with seating for 100 guests, overlooks the harbour and the local boating scene. Morning coffee before your boat trip, sandwiches made to order for your boat trip, welcome lunches after your boat trip – or assorted meals and drinks, even if you are not going on any boat trip, are all available here for individuals or groups! Coach tours – with advance booking – are also welcome.

Based at the visitor centre's waterfront pontoon dock, as at Portmagee's major marina facility across the harbour, a number of local passenger boats cater for Skellig visitors – four-and-a-half hour trips to land and visit on Skellig Michael or three-hour cruises to circumnavigate the islands. Such is the current demand, that already, in 2017, the visitor centre's car parking area – which was adequate for twenty-five years –

has been almost doubled in size, and the Centre's staff numbers have increased from an original seven in 1992 to twenty in 2017.

And, happily, in this busy tourism scene – as distinct from our humble, Knightstown-based Skellig trip of 1975 – (Chapter 4) – the customer demography now includes as many native-born Skellig enthusiasts as visitors from farther afield.

Skellig boats on stand-by at the Skellig Experience Visitor Centre.

Movie extras!

CHAPTER TEN

STAR WARS

First, it was only a 'whisper-and-a-nod' between a few boatmen who 'were in the know': 'Big news... A *Star Wars* movie is going to be shot on Skellig in July or August... Top secret... Don't mention a word... There'll be non-disclosure forms to be signed – an' all that... All the boats will be hired... And they'll be paid even if they never go to sea... Don't mention a word... Not a word'!

But sooner than you could say 'Jedi', the wildfire news spread from Portmagee to the farthest tip of Donegal – and to galaxies farther away! Suddenly every service provider – from boatman to butcher, baker and boutique was on overdrive, sensing the inevitable movie bonanza!

Having ferried poets, artists, writers, sensitive documentary makers and many, many thousands of appreciative visitors to Skellig over some forty summers in my faithful, 32' *Beal Bocht*, and having worked on the special effects crew of *Ryan's Daughter* in Dingle and Kilkee for eighteen months in 1968/70, the prospect of a few days' transport duty at Skellig with *Star Wars* in July 2014 was never going to be the highlight of my boating career. Nor was it going to interfere with my long-planned retirement date of September of that year.

As a consequence, from the outset, I tended to view the overall *Star Wars* razzmatazz through a slightly jaundiced eye.

Negotiators from the film industry had engaged with the Skellig boatmen quite some time in advance of the 2014 shooting date, and when financial agreement was eventually reached, it was reached in the knowledge that the Skellig would be closed to the public for the three-day duration of the shoot and that Skellig landing trips – many long-booked by eager visitors – could not be pursued. Nor could these bookings be converted to cruises around the island, because a two-mile exclusion zone around Skellig would be patrolled and enforced by the Irish navy. The official Marine Notification under the Maritime Safety Act 2005, cable-tied to the Portmagee marina gate, left nobody in any doubt: 'The Exclusion Zone is established in an area bounded by a 2 nautical mile circumference of Position 51*46.231' N, 010*32.415' W.'

Portmagee becomes Porgmagee to celebrate *The Last Jedi.*

What this deployment of the naval forces had to do with protecting the privacy of a commercial undertaking is still unclear, but who, among inshore boatmen in their eleven-metre boats was going to challenge the might of the 90-metre, 2256-ton L.E. *Samuel Beckett* at sea? Likewise, in the pandemic of 'confidentiality agreements' and in the presence of substantial private 'security' on pier, pontoon and parking lot, who was going to challenge this use of the Maritime Safety Act ashore?

One fearless journalist and his cameraman did set out to run the Skellig Exclusion Zone gauntlet in a fast RIB. A naval officer from the L.E.*Samuel Beckett* – in a faster RIB – intervened and stymied their chances. Nonetheless, where fresh *Star Wars* news releases were few, this high seas encounter, courteous in the extreme – and captured on video – became the top *Star Wars* news headline of the day for Paschal Sheehy of RTE.

Meanwhile, Skellig boats were active in assorted duties – some to ferry film personnel, some to ferry filming hardware, some to ferry lunches to the crew on Skellig, some to deliver – and retrieve – voluminous 'port-a-loos', and others stationed on safety stand-by at Skellig – yet initially forbidden by 'security' to tie-up in the shelter of the landing!

Daily, a limited number of helicopter flights shuttled stars and movie-makers between their Valentia base-camp and Skellig.

Many press and TV headlines – before and after the event – focussed on the overall management of the whole Skellig/*Star Wars* project by Government Departments and related bodies. For the casual reader or viewer, it was difficult to know who was responsible for the welfare of Skellig and who, in a melee of officialdom, carried – or should carry – the most influence in this event.

Concerned citizens had been asking questions from the outset: Had the relevant wildlife bodies been consulted, had UNESCO been consulted, had Birdwatch Ireland's initial criticism of the project been taken into account, had the Irish Film Board, which promoted the location, been even remotely aware of the sensitivity of the island's eco-structure or the EU's Birds and Habitat Directives, had any shortcuts been taken when the filming – originally planned for September – was brought forward to July to facilitate Lucas-Disney?

This too was the moment when An Taisce, national heritage watchdog of Ireland, might have spoken out strongly rather than delay its contribution until December 2017 when the deed was already done and the historical and natural heritage of Skellig was already being re-branded internationally by Fáilte Ireland and Tourism Ireland as some sort of a fantasy Disneyland theme park.

In a practical sense, most of the public concerns for Skellig architecture or wildlife had been overstated. Any film crew, shooting by day under the watchful eyes of the OPW's Skellig wardens could hardly create any more wear and tear to the monuments or any more upset to bird life than a normal day's complement of 180 visitors.

Puffins were not the least bit discommoded; any that wandered into an active filming scene on Skellig were subsequently digitally morphed into the cheeky squeaky porgs that featured in *The Last Jedi*.

Had night time operations been involved, the nocturnal birds – storm petrels and Manx shearwaters – both of which have long incubation and fledging periods – would be very vulnerable at that late July date. But, other than one late-evening homecoming of VIPs courtesy of the L.E.*Samuel Beckett*, Skellig and its relevant citizens had the *Star Wars*

THE
FORCE
PERFECT
PINT
CHALLENGE

the
Moorings
Portmagee

May the craic be with

PULL THE PERFECT PINT
LIKE THE JEDI MASTER MARK HAMILL

take up the challenge you must!

GUINNESS

GUINNESS

A shrine to Star Wars in the Moorings/Bridge bar at Portmagee.

nights to themselves.

Eventually, December 2015 saw the premiere of *Star Wars VII, The Force Awakens*, and in the related press euphoria of the following day I was but a very small voice by opining that this use of Skellig had 'reduced the island's status to a bit of set-dressing for a cartoon'.

December 2017 and a viewing of *Star Wars VIII, The Last Jedi*, left me equally despondent: Why the real Skellig, I wondered? Surely Lucas-Disney could have created an adequate 'Skellig' – computerised or physical – in a studio, particularly since the few minutes of Skellig scenes that appear at the end of *The Force Awakens* contain studio-created background islands that do not exist! Surely, again, Lucas-Disney could have fabricated – on any convenient clifftop – a glass-fibre version of Skellig monastery for *The Force Awakens* as they later did on West Kerry's Sybil Head (Ceann Sibeal) for supplementary scenes of *The Last Jedi?* And indeed, even though the *Irish Examiner*'s photo scoop of April 2016 clearly showed that this particular Sybil Head set bore no more than a fanciful resemblance to the Skellig monastery, who would notice the difference? And who – in worldwide audiences – would notice that most scenes of actor interaction 'on Skellig' were actually shot at the fabricated monastery on the Sybil Head set?

Can it be, I wondered, that the physical shooting on Skellig was more a publicity ploy than a necessary component of the work – a ruse to rejuvenate a weary movie theme of the 1970s by anchoring it to a vibrant Skellig World Heritage Site? Likewise, perhaps the plethora of 'confi-

dentiality agreements' we were asked to sign were no more than a titivation – a crafted bait to ensure leakage of the magical 'Skellig' word? Because adequate leakage there was!

Ploy or otherwise, nothing takes from the fact that *The Force Awak-ens* immediately awakened enormous

Left: At the Premiere; Des & unidentified Stormtrooper (Photo: Don MacMonagle. macmonagle.com)

Opposite: Standing over three metres tall, Skellig's Wailing Woman stone – part of the ancient penitential Stations of the Cross route – is still an iconic landmark on Skellig's Southern climb.

tourist activity with proportional financial rewards for the entire South Kerry area – and beyond. As a consequence, summer days of 2017 immediately saw Skellig passenger boats worked to the limit, restaurants full, pubs overflowing, waterfront parking lots crammed, record attendances at the Skellig Experience Visitor Centre, and 'No Vacancy' the common summer sight on every B&B accommodation. In a further testament to a new Skellig era, two of the latest vessels to join the Skellig fleet in 2017 bear the names *Skellig Walker* and *Force Awakens*!

But anyone who thought that South Kerry might bask quietly in such adequate *Star Wars* sunshine would be mistaken. March 2018 saw a further round of tourism promotions with Fáilte Ireland's announcement of a newly-adopted, three-day, *Star Wars* festival, 'May the Fourth be with You', to take place on 4th, 5th, and 6th May!

Be this a matter of taking a lead from Toronto's first such major *Star Wars* festival event in 2011, or be it an Irish creation of an Irish session, it drew enthusiastic attendances at a range of related local offerings – one being an opportunity to experience a virtual reality Skellig tour in a synthetic-built, four-metre-high 'Skellig' cell that had already featured in a tourism promotion in Berlin, the other being an outdoor, drive-in screening of *Star Wars* on Valentia Island's Bray head and on Ballyferriter's Béal Bán strand! The particular magic of these latter presentations lay in the fact that the Skelligs were in full view on the south side of the Bray head 'theatre', and in Ballyferriter, the broad expanse of Smerwick harbour and the steep slopes of The Three Sisters presented an equally stunning backdrop for the Béal Bán screening. Overall, 'The Fourth' created a welcome, pre-season tourism stimulant – not alone in the Skellig heartland, where an enthusiastic Portmagee underwent a festival-long name change to *PORGMAGEE*, but in every location on the *Wild Atlantic Way* where the affable, amiable filming personnel of *The Force Awakens* and *The Last Jedi* had set foot.

But apart from festivities, apart from promotions, apart from headcounts, apart from visitor-interest analyses and apart from buoyant tourism incomes, the local reality is that the Skellig Michael of old, faithfully married to monasticism for fifteen hundred years, must – for the moment – sleep restlessly in a forced celebrity marriage – a 'made match' – with Luke Skywalker, Rey, and those multiple alien bedfellows of *Star Wars VII* and *VIII* – including porgs and crystal foxes!

The wedding dowry – directly into Ireland's purse - is potentially enormous. And the upsurge in local tourism in the immediate aftermath of the *Star Wars VII* release was but the down payment! It is worth noting that *Ryan's Daughter* (1969), still brings fans to the Dingle peninsula seeking out the locations where Rosy Ryan (Sarah Miles) and the war-damaged Major Randolph Doryan (Christopher Jones) held their illicit trysts. Likewise, the shenanigans of Sean Thornton and Mary Kate Danaher,

(John Wayne and Maureen O'Hara), in *The Quiet Man* (1952) still generate theme tourism in that Galway/Mayo hinterland. By this yardstick, the Skellig islands and their South Kerry surroundings – including Portmagee's Bridge Bar – now a virtual *Star Wars* shrine where *Star Wars'* Mark Hamill famously learned to pull a pint of Guinness – must equally be on the itinerary of every true *Star Wars* follower from near and far and from present to future.

Accepting, however, that movie theme followers worldwide shall ever differ, some sceptics will rate *Star Wars* as nonsense; true adherents in the millions shall relish its mayhem, blow by blow by blow.

But the liberties taken by the script writers of *Star Wars VIII* went one blow too far: Irrespective of the nonsense or the splendour of the overall work, Rey's light-sabre-destruction of Skellig's iconic Wailing Woman stone, fictional though it may be, constituted the ultimate Skellig disrespect, a gratuitous act of sacrilege in a UNESCO shrine to Irish history and culture – the epitome, perhaps, of what the concerned citizens had feared at the outset.

But time may heal the pain: While noting earlier that folklorists of today still mention the 5th century tale, when Duagh, King of West Munster, fleeing for his life from the King of Cashel, sought the sanctuary of Skellig, few would expect Luke Skywalker's Skellig exile to be similarly featured in folk tales 1,500 years hence.

Wind, rain, ocean, earthquake and time ever conspire to bring the islands to their knees.

CHAPTER ELEVEN

100 YEARS FROM NOW

Such are the Skellig Rocks – Skellig Michael and Small Skellig – not our properties, but nonetheless our individual and collective responsibilities.

In the original edition of this book, (O'Brien Press, Ltd. 1976), an era when it was difficult to gather together half a dozen souls who had ever even heard of Skellig, I posed a question: 'What does the future hold for these islands, ten, fifty, one hundred years from now?'

The fifty-year answer is already becoming clear: On 12th July 2017, some five hundred passengers visited the Skelligs on some forty-five boat trips!

Of those passengers, one hundred and eighty landed on Skellig Michael as per the OPW'S current fifteen boat landing permit programme.

The remaining hundreds were glad to avail of the alternative – a cruise around the Skelligs to gaze thereupon in awe…

Credit this increase in Skellig-related footfall to many sources:

Fáilte Ireland's creation and widespread publicity of the Wild Atlantic Way rerouted a new swathe of visitors to the Atlantic coastal counties, and the South Kerry area, where Skellig is a 'Discovery' point, undoubtedly received its share.

In the heart of the region – Valentia, Portmagee, Finian's Bay and Ballinskelligs – further local advertising incentives took hold:

The Skellig Ring, The Valentia Ring and the Dark Skies Region all combined to attract and retain visitors in the immediate area.

Medieval doorway in the mainland monastery at Ballinskelligs.

Likewise, at the extremes of the region – from Kells to Castlecove – the Skellig Coast Discovery area ties-in Skellig-related themes from Dingle bay and Kenmare Bay, and in return, carries the precious Skellig name farther afield. Other beneficial sources of promotion are many and varied: Kerry County Development Plan 2015-2021, Kerry County Tourism Strategy 2016-2020, South Kerry LEADER Local Development Strategy 2014-2020, and the Wild Atlantic Way Operational Programme 2015-2019... All the while, the long-standing promotion of the age-old Ring of Kerry provides an endless stream of visitors to the overall area, and, looking to the future, Tourism Ireland's 2016 launch of a specially commissioned video with input from Star Wars personnel, is destined for fourteen new markets abroad.

As a further coincidence with these general promotions, a switch from print to online marketing by local Skellig stakeholders began to bear the fruit of splendid websites, extolling the sights, sounds and experiences of Skellig in word, photograph and video.

And then came *Star Wars*! The advertising might of Hollywood added multiples of fuel to an already glowing fire, and presented the Skellig region, Kerry county – and Ireland as a whole – with a publicity benefit that is quite incalculable!

A glance through any newspaper or website report, local or international, since the Skellig and *Star Wars* story broke in 2014, will find spectacular headline coverage of this science-fiction epic and its incredible location:

'*Remote Irish Island to feature in Star Wars.*' (theguardian.com)
'*In a galaxy not so far away... Skellig takes a leading role in new Star*

Wars film.' (independent.ie)

'Skellig Michael, un viaje al mundo de Star Wars' (elfinanciero.com)

'Return of the Jedi: Star Wars Episode VIII goes back to Skellig Michael.' (theguardian.com)

'Spoiler Alert: This island appears in Star Wars' (nytimes.com)

'Ireland awaits Star Wars tourists at Skellig Michael' (montrealgazette. com)

'L'incanto dell'Irlanda del set di Star Wars' (repubblica.it)

'Just indescribably beautiful': Star Wars cast describe Skellig Michael.' (irishtimes.com)

Not since 1996 did the Skelligs come to such international prominence. Its designation in that year as a UNESCO World Heritage Site may not have yielded any comparable lionisation, but it achieved something more. It stirred the conscience as to the welfare of the island compared to the forces aligned against it: nature, time and human interference.

Nature knows no mercy, no remorse; the ancient stonework of the monastic site, the access stairways, and the artery that is the lighthouse road, are ever at the mercy or whim of the elements. Several serious rock falls on to the roadway can be linked to the excessive rainfall of recent years, resulting in closure of the island during repairs and remedial safety work. The road near Cross Cove has long been roofed as a protection against frequent showers of stones and rubble unearthed by puffins and rabbits in the slopes above. But a roof is scant remedy when tons of rock tumble down a near-vertical cliff.

Human visitation on Skellig Michael has also been a concern in many minds – particularly among the policy makers and administrators of the OPW. The question posed today is this: Can the ancient structures, which braved the Viking attacks of the Middle Ages and endured several years of habitation – and various alterations – by the lighthouse builders of the 1820s, survive today's tourist traffic and go unscathed?

Visitor attendance figures, inevitably attached to all or any Skellig news bulletins, create an impression of crowds jostling for space and trampling the island into the sea. This is not the case; the well-policed attendance is 180 visitors a day. And the 180 visitors of tomorrow, or many tomorrows, under the watchful eyes of the OPW'S resident wardens, shall hardly create any more wear and tear than the 180 of today?

In another querulous vein, the oft-quoted comparisons of the low annual counts of early years with the higher attendance figures of today carry an inference that an increase is not a desirable development... This impression is reinforced by the OPW'S imposition, since 2007, of a curtailed Skellig 'season' from mid May to end of September.

This restriction, since its inception, has been partially hidden in the OPW'S argument that due to weather conditions Skellig cannot be readily accessed for timely pre or post-season maintenance.

Yet, according to an independent study of twenty-five years of data, April and October can, on average, offer respectively 15 days and 14 days of Skellig-fit sea conditions – a period adequate for all normal maintenance, claim the boatmen.

Submissions and interventions by local public representatives supporting a restoration of the full April-October season seem destined to be but pipe dreams: In August 2017, Kevin Moran, the then Minister of State with responsibility for the OPW, flatly turned down proposals for a restoration of the full Skellig season, saying that the OPW would 'robustly limit the footfall on Skellig Michael.'

But hopes were raised again only three months later when - on October 3ʳᵈ 2017 - the OPW announced a Review of the length of the Skellig Michael visitor season and sought input from the Skellig Boatmen's Group, the Skellig Architectural Team, the OPW Depot manager, the Department of Culture, Heritage & Gaeltacht, Visitor Services and Failte Ireland!

The communiqué also promised an early decision, 'before the end of 2017'. But the deadline passed - as did January, February and March. And when the 2018 opening date was finally announced, it was still mid May as before!

Meanwhile, aspects of access to Skellig Michael are becoming clearer to the public eye: All boatmen, provided that they - and their vessels - comply with the modern standards and certification of the Department of Transport, are eligible to apply in a triennial public competition for the OPW's Skellig landing permits - still limited to fifteen. It is a wide-ranging specification, taking account of the seafaring and Skellig-related experience of skipper and crew, as well as the provision of such on-board safety equipment and material comforts as may be expected by the passengers of this age.

But these considerations are only the little affairs of humans. While the eventual, mainland home of the Skellig monastic community is but a muted Medieval ruin on the shores of Ballinskelligs Bay, its Early Christian forebear, Skellig Michael, still defies time - and revels annually in the rebirth of its beautiful oceanic soul in the form of puffins and petrels and gannets and guillemots and sharks and seals and summer skies and shining silver seas.

It is a permanent portion of heaven, too wonderful to lock up, too precious to neglect, too fragile to endure the least tampering, and crying out for a real Solomon who can wisely chart its future course, as wind, rain, ocean, earthquake, time, gravity and, yes, footfall itself, ever conspire to bring the island to its knees.

But where is that Solomon? A major RTE documentary, *Great Lighthouses of Ireland*, on October 21st 2018, referred to the 2017/18 repair and restoration of the long-disused road between the current Skellig lighthouse and the higher, old, ruined North Station, mentioning that 'when this work is complete, the ruins of the upper lighthouse will be repaired and made safe for visitors'.

What visitors, one must ask. An additional (hurried) tour for the monastery visitors? An optional, alternative 'lighthouse' tour? A tour for special guests? And who can administer such an additional tour with only the existing OPW staff numbers, the existing Skellig opening hours and the existing Skellig boat services?

Those of us who have known an older Skellig intimately in the past are privileged indeed. Those of us who shall see Skellig in the future must do so with awe, respect and reverence.

And those of us who have Skellig imprinted in their very genes must ask again – this time with rather more disquiet – 'What does the future hold for these islands, ten, fifty, one hundred years from now'?

Skellig sunset.